ANCHOR POINTS

ANCHOR POINTS

REVIEW AND HERALD® PUBLISHING ASSOCIATION
HAGERSTOWN, MD 21740

Scripture quotations marked NASB are from the *New American Standard Bible*, © The Lockman
Foundation 1960, 1962, 1963, 1968, 1971, 1972, 1973, 1975, 1977.

Texts credited to NIV are from the *Holy Bible, New International Version.* Copyright © 1973,
1978, 1984, International Bible Society. Used by permission of Zondervan Bible Publishers.

Texts credited to NKJV are from The New King James Version. Copyright © 1979, 1980, 1982,
Thomas Nelson, Inc., Publishers.

Bible texts credited to NRSV are from the New Revised Standard Version of the Bible, copyright
© 1989 by the Division of Christian Education of the National Council of the Churches of Christ
in the U.S.A. Used by permission.

Bible texts credited to RSV are from the Revised Standard Version of the Bible, copyright © 1946,
1952, 1971, by the Division of Christian Education of the National Council of the Churches of
Christ in the U.S.A. Used by permission.

Verses marked TLB are taken from *The Living Bible,* copyright © 1971 by Tyndale House
Publishers, Wheaton, Ill. Used by permission.

Coordinating editor, Penny Estes Wheeler
Designed by Bill Kirstein
Cover design by Helcio Deslandes
Type set: Century School Book 11/13

PRINTED IN U.S.A.

98 97 96 95 94 93   10 9 8 7 6 5 4 3 2 1

R & H Cataloging Service

Anchorpoints.

  1. Seventh-day Adventists—Doctrinal and controversial works.
I. Johnsson, William George, 1934-   II. Adventist Review.
III. Title: Anchor points.
        286.73

ISBN 0-8280-0720-9

Contents

Introduction

By William G. Johnsson

Late in 1991 the *Adventist Review* editors spent many hours in concentrated planning for the church paper. As we assessed the state of the Seventh-day Adventist Church in North America and overseas, we saw dangers of polarization on the horizon.

On one side we observed tendencies to water down core teachings and practices; on the other, a move in the opposite direction, a separation in reaction to the first trend. In either case the result would be weakening and fragmentation of the church.

Those discussions highlighted the need for a major new thrust of the *Adventist Review*. The *Review* must be used of God to help draw Adventists together, calling us all back to our core teachings, mission, lifestyle, and hope. Those great ideas that made us a distinct movement 150 years ago—we must go back to them.

But not merely go back: we must show how the fundamental truths that shaped us impact life today. We didn't want to have principally history or a set of Bible doctrines, although sound history and theology must undergird the presentations. No; we wanted something fresh and contemporary, but solidly grounded in our heritage.

So we had the concept, but how to convey it? What phrase, what word might capture it? Could we find a term that would encapsulate our plans and that would also lend itself to visual portrayal?

We brainstormed ideas over several sessions, brainstormed until we had explored scores of phrases and words and our heads ached, and still we came up dry.

I remember the morning I said to the others, "Let's not spend any more energy on this. What these presentations *say* will be more important than what we call them."

And then suddenly we had "AnchorPoints." Out of the blue (the divine blue) it was there. It was as though the Lord could come through for us only when we had exhausted our best efforts.

AnchorPoints—you won't find the term in a dictionary or thesaurus. But it was just what we wanted.

We sought out the best writers in the church for AnchorPoints: not just scholars, but those who can write clearly and attractively and who have struggled to apply faith to life. We wanted younger writers whenever possible. We sent out invitations, and not one person refused.

And the response to AnchorPoints? Overwhelming! These treatments, which we always give first place in an issue, have brought a uniformly positive response. They have been quoted, reprinted, and discussed.

"We have this hope as an anchor for the soul, firm and secure," says Scripture (Heb. 6:19, NIV). We praise our God for Jesus, Anchor of all our hopes, and we seek to give Him all glory through AnchorPoints.

The Son

God the eternal Son became incarnate in Jesus Christ. Through Him all things were created, the character of God is revealed, the salvation of humanity is accomplished, and the world is judged. Forever truly God, He became also truly man, Jesus the Christ. He was conceived of the Holy Spirit and born of the virgin Mary. He lived and experienced temptation as a human being, but perfectly exemplified the righteousness and love of God. By His miracles He manifested God's power and was attested as God's promised Messiah. He suffered and died voluntarily on the cross for our sins and in our place, was raised from the dead, and ascended to minister in the heavenly sanctuary in our behalf. He will come again in glory for the final deliverance of His people and the restoration of all things. (John 1:1-3, 14; Col. 1:15-19; John 10:30; 14:9; Rom. 6:23; 2 Cor. 5:17-19; John 5:22; Luke 1:35; Phil. 2:5-11; Heb. 2:9-18; 1 Cor. 15:3, 4; Heb. 8:1, 2; John 14:1-3.)—
Fundamental Beliefs, *No. 4.*

CHAPTER ONE

By William G. Johnsson

Jesus
Center of All Our Hopes

O f all the names given children since the dawn of time, one stands alone, solitary, immovable. Although many men and women now take that name in oath or jest, one day every knee in heaven and earth will bow before Him who bears it and declare that He is King of kings and Lord of lords. That name is the sweetest sound to come from infant lips; it sustains us through life; and it will be our security when we embark on our final journey.

Jesus.

All our hopes—for this world and the next—center in Him. Our best joys, our highest aspirations, our cleanest motivations, spring from Him. Every other name will pass away; His, never.

When we conceived the idea of AnchorPoints—fundamentals of faith that transform contemporary life—we first planned to begin with the Bible. Indeed, that would make good sense; the Scriptures, God's Word, provide the source of all spiritual knowledge. But in the final analysis Jesus, not the Bible, is our chief AnchorPoint. He, the Eternal Word, called forth the Written Word; that Word, which testifies of Him (John 5:39), finds its meaning only in Him.

So let the message go out: At the center of Adventist faith stands a Person, not a creed or set of rules. Jesus anchors our hopes.

Jesus will be the theme of our praise throughout eternity. The whole world could not contain the books that might be written about Him (John 21:25); what then can we accomplish in one short chapter? We at least can address four issues of concern to Adventists today: Who is He? What did He do? What does He mean to us? And wherein, if at all, do Adventists understand Jesus in ways different from other Christians?

Who Is Jesus?

Jesus Himself raised the question: " 'But what about you?' he asked. 'Who do you say I am?' " (Matt. 16:15).*

The question has haunted millions across the centuries, just as it haunts men and women today. This Man of lowly birth, this Carpenter of Nazareth, this itinerant Preacher-Healer whom the Romans crucified—who was He? Jesus won't go away; His question won't go away.

An amazing thing about this Jesus is that the plaudits we use to exalt others demean this Man. A good man? A great man? Prophet? Martyr? The best person who ever lived? Say any or all of these about Jesus, and you do not honor Him—you sell Him short.

For He claimed to be more. He saw Himself not merely man, but as the Son of man. This, His preferred designation, suggests representative man and connects with the visions related in Daniel 7:13-15 and Ezekiel 2:1, 3, 6, 8, etc.

Paul, perhaps picking up on this idea, calls Jesus the Second Adam (1 Cor. 15:45). Jesus stands at the head of a new line, a new race, a new humanity that reverses all that was lost in the first Adam.

Like Adam, Jesus of Nazareth was flesh and blood (Heb. 2:14). Fully and truly human, He suffered heat and cold, pain and hunger, sorrow and temptation, and at last death itself.

But the biblical witness and the testimony of those who knew Jesus goes beyond—Jesus was *more* than a man. When Peter exclaimed "You are the Christ, the Son of the living God," Jesus did not correct him. Instead He said: "Blessed are you, Simon son of Jonah, for this was not revealed to you by man, but by my Father in heaven" (Matt. 16:16, 17).

Jesus had no human father. The Holy Spirit came upon the virgin Mary, so that the child of her womb was both God and man. Immanuel—God with us (Matt. 1:20-23). "And without controversy great is the mystery of godliness: God was manifest in the

10

flesh, justified in the Spirit, seen of angels, preached unto the Gentiles, believed on in the world, received up into glory" (1 Tim. 3:16, KJV).

Here, then, is the scandal of Christianity: that in the Carpenter of Nazareth the eternal God has come to earth, has entered into time and taken a body. He has pitched His tent in our midst, has entered into our lostness and brokenness and become one of us. "In the beginning was the Word, and the Word was with God, and the Word was God. . . . The Word became flesh and lived for a while among us" (John 1:1-14).

Jesus. The scandal of His name. The scandal of His claim. But to those who believe, He is precious, chosen by God, our Cornerstone (1 Peter 2:4-7).

Reader, what about you? Whom do *you* say He is?

What Did Jesus Do?

Never a person spoke like Jesus (John 7:46); never a person lived like Jesus. "He went around doing good" (Acts 10:38)—healing the sick, bringing good news to the poor, blessing the children, feeding the hungry, raising the dead.

What a life! A life of gentleness and kindness, of nobility and honesty. A life that flowed out to lift everyone within its orbit. A life that burned with justice and equity, conferring dignity and self-respect upon Gentiles and women, harlots and tax collectors.

What a life! Such purity of word and motive, of speech and deed; so unselfish, so giving, so compassionate. " 'He committed no sin, and no deceit was found in his mouth.' When they hurled their insults at him, he did not retaliate; when he suffered, he made no threats" (1 Peter 2:22, 23).

Yet as exemplary as was His life, the New Testament writers put the emphasis elsewhere. The four Gospels focus on His passion—the closing events leading up to Calvary. Throughout His ministry Jesus tried to prepare His followers for what lay ahead in Jerusalem; He spoke of His "hour" that would soon come.

He came to Jerusalem for the last time. Hailed as Israel's king on Sunday and led in exultant procession, He was arrested in stealth on Thursday night, sentenced by a kangaroo court, and executed the next day. And it was Passover.

By any normal reckoning, Jesus' followers should have been shamed by His dying. The Romans reserved crucifixion for the vilest of criminals, and Jesus was crucified. But Christians did not try to conceal the cross, nor did they apologize for it. Rather, they *exalted* the cross. "But God forbid that I should glory, save in the cross of our Lord Jesus Christ, by whom the world is crucified unto me, and I unto the world" (Gal. 6:14, KJV). "For I determined not to know any thing among you, save Jesus Christ, and him crucified" (1 Cor. 2:2, KJV).

The scandal of Jesus' work: He died on a cross. But, says the Scripture, just as *God* was in this Man Jesus—in His birth, life, and ministry—so *God* was in His death. Jesus' death meant no failure; *au contraire,* it marked the crown of His achievement. By His dying, God entered our experience of woe and hopelessness, our guilt and despair, our death. God entered, took it upon Himself, and delivered us (1 Peter 2:24, 25; 2 Cor. 5:18, 19).

"Christ was treated as we deserve, that we might be treated as He deserves. He was condemned for our sins, in which He had no share, that we might be justified by His righteousness, in which we had no share. He suffered the death which was ours, that we might receive the life which was His. 'With his stripes we are healed' " (*The Desire of Ages,* p. 25).

Our assurance is not in what we are, but in what He is; not in what we have done, but in what He has done. We are complete in Him (Col. 2:10); He is our righteousness, our holiness, our redemption (1 Cor. 1:30).

Calvary was the fulcrum of the ages. There Jesus, God's Son, won the great battle, ensured the final triumph of truth and right; there He offered Himself a living sacrifice, perfect and complete, to take away the sins of the world (John 1:29). Nothing can ever, need ever, be added to what He accomplished there.

But Jesus' work for us did not end at Calvary. Risen from the tomb, He ministers in the heavenly courts as our great high priest (Heb. 8:1, 2). The judge of all, He soon will come again, not to deal with sin, but to receive His dominion and His people (Heb. 9:27, 28). Concerning these great truths, we will study more in later AnchorPoints.

Jesus. That name gives us hope. Our future, in this life and beyond, rests upon what we do with this Man who died on a cross. "For God so loved the world, that he gave his only begotten Son, that whosoever believeth in him should not perish, but have everlasting life" (John 3:16, KJV).

What Jesus Means Today

Jesus made all the difference when He was on earth; He still does, if we will let Him.

• *He is alive!* We may know Him, walk with Him, have Him as our friend. "Though you have not seen him, you love him; and even though you do not see him now, you believe in him and are filled with an inexpressible and glorious joy, for you are receiving the goal of your faith, the salvation of your souls" (1 Peter 1:8, 9).

Jesus is the best friend we can ever know. He will never fail us, never turn on us, never leave us. We can trust Him.

Those who take Jesus at His word find in their experience that what He said about Himself is true. He *is* the Messiah, the Son of the living God. He *is* the Saviour of the world, and my Saviour, too.

• *Discovering who we are.* By discovering Jesus, we discover ourselves. Only through seeing Him do we see who we are and what we might be.

Seeing Him, we see our rottenness, our smallness, our pettiness, our gross selfishness. We see how far we fall short of God's ideal. But we also see His hand stretched out in love to receive us, to lift us out of the pit, to clothe us with the garments of salvation.

So we catch a vision of God's plan for us. We discover that God loves us and has a plan for our lives, that He is concerned with the quality of human life, that He wants to spend quality time with us. "Behold, what manner of love the Father hath bestowed upon us, that we should be called the sons of God: therefore the world knoweth us not, because it knew him not. Beloved, now are we the sons of God, and it doth not yet appear what we shall be: but we know that, when he shall appear, we shall be like him; for we shall see him as he is" (1 John 3:1, 2, KJV). "Higher than the highest human thought can reach is God's ideal for His children. Godliness—godlikeness—is the goal to be reached" (*Education*, p. 18).

• *Life in the Jesus lane.* Life in the Jesus lane is life trans-

13

formed. It's life with meaning and purpose, life with zest and energy. "The thief comes only to steal and kill and destroy; I have come that they may have life, and have it to the full" (John 10:10). That promise still works.

"And my God will meet all your needs according to his glorious riches in Christ Jesus" (Phil. 4:19). "He who did not spare his own Son, but gave him up for us all—how will he not also, along with him, graciously give us all things?" (Rom. 8:32).

How Adventists Understand Jesus

These affirmations about Jesus—His person and His work—place Adventists in the solid, biblical center of Christian tradition. Of course, not all who might be classified as "Christian" share them today—for instance, liberals who reject His deity or fringe groups that hold that He was created in long-distant time.

Indeed, some early Adventists held to the latter view, which is of ancient origin. But Ellen White in particular emphasized His eternal preexistence in unequivocal language: "In Christ is life, original, unborrowed, underived" (*The Desire of Ages,* p. 530).

Today some Adventists argue over the humanity of Jesus: Was His nature exactly like ours—with our sinful tendencies—or not? Whatever view we may hold on this point, however, Adventist faith makes the following affirmations: (1) Jesus was fully God; (2) Jesus was fully human; (3) the divine and human natures were blended in one person; (4) His sufferings and temptations were real, with the possibility of failure; and (5) Jesus was without sin, a perfect Saviour.

Do Adventists, then, have any understanding of Jesus that is unique?

None that is unique; but in two of our emphases we retain perspectives that have almost wholly dropped away from other denominations.

First, we understand Jesus' person and work in the context of His great controversy with Satan. The canvas for the plan of salvation is broad, extending from the time before Creation to the restoration of all things.

Second, we study Christ's post-cross work. His ministry in the heavenly sanctuary. This work does not add anything to the efficacy of His atoning death, but it shows that He is active on behalf of His people today as events rush on to their climax.

Both of these ideas will form future AnchorPoints. But whatever AnchorPoint we take up, we want Jesus to be center. We look for Bible-based presentations that touch life today, but most of all, "we would like to see Jesus" (John 12:21). For "worthy is the Lamb, who was slain, to receive power and wealth and wisdom and strength and honor and glory and praise!" (Rev. 5:12).

---

* Unless otherwise noted, Bible references in this chapter are from the New International Version.

Born in Australia, Dr. William G. Johnsson has been a chemist, missionary, teacher, administrator, author, and editor. He served for 15 years in India before going to the Seventh-day Adventist Seminary at Andrews University, where he taught New Testament and served as associate dean. From there he went to the *Adventist Review* as associate editor. Upon the retirement of Kenneth Wood in 1982, he became editor. His hobbies include long-distance running and gardening.

Christ's Ministry in the Heavenly Sanctuary

There is a sanctuary in heaven, the true tabernacle which the Lord set up and not man. In it Christ ministers on our behalf, making available to believers the benefits of His atoning sacrifice offered once for all on the cross. He was inaugurated as our great High Priest and began His intercessory ministry at the time of His ascension. In 1844, at the end of the prophetic period of 2300 days, He entered the second and last phase of His atoning ministry. It is a work of investigative judgment which is part of the ultimate disposition of all sin, typified by the cleansing of the ancient Hebrew sanctuary on the Day of Atonement. In that typical service the sanctuary was cleansed with the blood of animal sacrifices, but the heavenly things are purified with the perfect sacrifice of the blood of Jesus. The investigative judgment reveals to heavenly intelligences who among the dead are asleep in Christ and therefore, in Him, are deemed worthy to have part in the first resurrection. It also makes manifest who among the living are abiding in Christ, keeping the commandments of God and the faith of Jesus, and in Him, therefore, are ready for translation into His everlasting kingdom. This judgment vindicates the justice of God in saving those who believe in Jesus. It declares that those who have remained loyal to God shall receive the kingdom. The completion of this ministry of Christ will mark the close of human probation before the Second Advent. (Heb. 8:1-5; 4:14-16; 9:11-28; 10:19-22; 1:3; 2:16, 17; Dan. 7:9-27; 8:13, 14; 9:24-27; Num. 14:34; Eze. 4:6; Lev. 16; Rev. 14:6, 7; 20:12; 14:12; 22:12.)—
Fundamental Beliefs, *No. 23.*

CHAPTER TWO

By *Martin Weber*

Heaven on Our Side

Looking at the
Pre-Advent Judgment

A while back some friends and I formed a study group and—modestly—referred to ourselves as the "Last Hope of the Church Committee." All in good fun. The subjects we discussed month by month, however, were very serious.

One evening we met in my living room to debate the judgment of 1844 in the heavenly sanctuary. Perhaps we had our Bibles open. Our minds, however, were closed, and we didn't seem to be getting anywhere.

Finally one of my friends turned to me in exasperation: "Tell me honestly, what difference does it make? I know I'm accepted in Christ—so what does it matter whether or not there's a judgment going on in heaven now?"

A Hot Potato

The 1844 judgment has become a scorching hot potato in some circles in the Adventist Church. And much is at stake, since our sanctuary message is part of the doctrinal foundation of the church. If you do away with the sanctuary and the judgment, you undermine our biblical mandate for existence. We might as well be Seventh-day Baptists.

Who can deny that the devil has aimed his sharpest arrows at the sanctuary and the 1844 judgment? Yet I find it shocking how few Adventists are able to defend this doctrine from the Bible alone. When confronted with honest, probing questions about 1844, they quickly drop their Bibles and resort to the writings of Ellen White.

17

Thank God for the prophetic gift given to our church. But let's not abuse it. If we take our prophet seriously, we will accept her admonition to make the Bible our only rule of faith and doctrine. Everything we present as testing truth must be provable from the Scriptures. Otherwise, we make ourselves seem like a nonbiblical cult.

Other members seeking to establish a biblical foundation for their faith quietly dismiss the 1844 judgment. To them it's Jesus yes, judgment no. They regard themselves as enlightened Adventists, liberated from legalism.

My own assessment is that Satan has used legalism as a sledgehammer to dismantle faith in the sanctuary. And he has succeeded smashingly. For example, what comes to mind when you think of the Most Holy Place, the second compartment of the earthly sanctuary? Automatically you think of the law, right? How come? Was not all the action in the Most Holy Place over the mercy seat—that slab of gold on which the blood was sprinkled? Did not God specifically say that He would meet with His people from above the mercy seat (see Ex. 25:22)? Then why do we tend to think only of the law in connection with the Second Apartment?

At the Mercy Seat

The fact is that God cannot relate to unworthy sinners on the basis of how well we are fulfilling His law. He must meet with us at the mercy seat. After a century and a half of claiming to proclaim the truth about the sanctuary, I'd say it's about time we got that straight, don't you think? It's high time we flushed away all that legalism and preached the pure gospel truth about the sanctuary.

I remember my days as a child in church and church school. The goal of those over me was good behavior motivated by an incessant bombardment of guilt and fear: "Unless you become absolutely perfect in character, you cannot be saved when Jesus comes. Even now your name might have come up in judgment, and you might already be past the close of probation." Several classmates were convinced that their probation was past and that they had committed the unpardonable sin. "What's the use even trying?" they would lament. So they gave up hope and gave up on

18

God. More than 20 years later most of them are out of the church. Thanks to legalism. What a shame!

Steep Stairs

Other students, myself included, gritted their teeth and kept climbing those steep stairs to absolute perfection. We hoped someday to deserve being saved by grace. Unfortunately, everything we did for God was corrupted by guilt and fear, amounting to nothing but dead works. Jesus said, "If you *love* Me, keep My commandments" (John 14:15, NKJV). "There is *no fear in love;* but perfect love casts out fear, because fear involves torment. But he who fears has not been made perfect in love" (1 John 4:18, NKJV).

It should not surprise us that some Adventists seeking spiritual security have rejected the whole concept of a celestial pre-Advent judgment. They wonder, "Why should we who are already 'accepted in the Beloved' have to face the scrutiny of judgment? Didn't Jesus Himself say that 'he who hears My word and believes in Him who sent Me has everlasting life, and shall not come into judgment' [John 5:24, NKJV]?"

"No," protest the defenders of the faith. "Our King James Bible teaches that believers *are* judged. We escape 'condemnation,' but there is still a judgment all must face."

Then those who reject the pre-Advent judgment inform us that the King James, while normally reliable, is inconsistent here. In John 5:22 the Greek noun *krisis* is correctly translated "judgment," but two verses later the same word in the same context is changed to "condemnation." Even that favorite Adventist passage, Revelation 14, employs *krisis* to proclaim that "the hour of his judgment is come" (verse 7). Not the hour of His condemnation— His judgment. A judgment that, apparently according to the words of Jesus, does not involve believers.

The late Walter Martin, who was the world's foremost authority on cults, charged that "in John 5:24 the Greek deals a devastating blow to the Seventh-day Adventist concept of investigative judgment." Can we ignore the challenge of this evangelical Goliath?

Those who dismiss Adventist doctrine press their point with another perplexing passage: "He who believes in Him is *not*

19

judged" (John 3:18, NASB). "This only makes sense," they assert. "Why must God spend more than a century investigating records when already 'the Lord knows those who are His' [2 Tim. 2:19, NASB]?".

These questions bring considerable consternation. Usually we try to escape them by finding refuge in those safe and familiar passages that cement our doctrinal structure, texts like James 2:12: "So speak and so do as those who will be judged by the law of liberty" (RSV). "The work of Christ," we contend, "does not release us from accountability. We are told to 'give an account of your stewardship' [Luke 16:2]. Wherever there is accountability, there is judgment. Paul warns that 'we must all appear before the judgment seat of Christ' [2 Cor. 5:10]. Surely these scriptures all show that Christians must face judgment."

"Wait a minute!" another challenge intrudes. "You can't quote Paul to prove the investigative judgment. He tells us Christ is the judge. You say He's your defense attorney. How can Jesus both judge believers and represent them at the same time? You can't have it both ways."

Oh, well. Back to Revelation 14. In verse 7 it clearly states that during earth's final gospel proclamation "the hour of His judgment *has* come" (NASB).

And so it goes. Honest seekers of truth, thoroughly confused, wonder what to do.

For a while I found myself perplexed about questions like these. Now I'm so happy to have them completely settled in my mind. I can testify that the gospel truth about a judgment going on in the heavenly sanctuary inspires me with hope, assurance, and confidence.

How My Eyes Opened

The key to my new understanding was the ancient Hebrew meaning of judgment, which I found to be quite different from the legal system prevalent in Western countries today. The Western system requires judges and juries to be strictly neutral—to harbor no bias either in favor of or against the accused.

The *Jewish Encyclopedia* explains, however, that "attorneys at law are unknown in Jewish law." [1] Their legal code required judges to "[lean] always to the side of the defendant and give him the advantage of every possible doubt."[2]

Witnesses of the crime pressed charges, while the judge promoted the cause of the defendant, biased in favor of acquittal.[3] But the judge also had to execute justice. And if evidence of guilt could not be controverted, he would reluctantly abandon his defense of the accused and pronounce condemnation. But the point is that the entire system in ancient biblical times was predisposed toward *vindication,* not condemnation.

A wonderful concept. But it leaves us with a question: if God is defending us in the heavenly judgment, who would dare withstand Him? Actually, it's the devil who raises questions about our salvation in the judgment. The Bible calls him the "accuser of our brethren," who accuses us "before our God day and night" (Rev. 12:10).

Now, in certain situations the Hebrew judge appointed an advocate to assist him in defending the accused. The *Jewish Encyclopedia* states that the husband could represent his wife and help the judge defend her if the verdict involved his personal rights.[4]

Here we have a thrilling parallel with the heavenly judgment. Christ, bridegroom of the church, purchased us with His precious blood. Now He serves as our court-appointed advocate to help the Father defend us from Satan—and to defend His own claim to us.

Wonderful news! God in the judgment takes our side against Satan. Jesus, our advocate, assists by interceding for us. God finds in Jesus' sacrifice the legal basis to accept repenting sinners and count us perfect. I like that, don't you? It makes me feel confident about my salvation in Christ!

Now we see how Jesus, our judge, can also serve as our defender. There is no conflict in His dual role. It is, in fact, necessary for Jesus to defend us as our judge.

Another evidence of God's love for His children is shown by a further provision of the Hebrew legal system: "In the nature of things some parties cannot plead for themselves. Infants, boys under 13 or girls under 12, the deaf and dumb, and lunatics can plead only through a guardian; and it is the duty of the court to appoint a guardian for such, if they have none."[5]

Likewise, we are helpless, unable to defend ourselves from the devil's accusations. So God appoints Jesus, our sympathetic high priest, to intercede for us against the vicious charges of our adversary.

Back in 1980, when I first understood this good news about the judgment and the sanctuary, the Lord gave me a special illustration. I was standing in a supermarket checkout line leaning on a grocery cart when the realization suddenly struck me. Here I was waiting confidently in the checkout line, without any doubts that the groceries were going to be mine—this despite the fact that there was a judgment of sorts to pass before I could take the goods home.

You see, the clerk had to decide if I was "worthy" of having the groceries. And what was it that qualified me? It was the money I had in my hand. With cash to present to the clerk, the groceries would unquestionably be mine to take home.

Celestial Checkout

Heaven's judgment is something like that. Jesus is the treasure we need to pass the celestial checkout. With Jesus we can be assured of a favorable verdict, whatever our sincere struggles may be. God isn't threatened by our faults and failures. Just as the grocery store decided beforehand that whoever has money qualifies for groceries, God has declared that everyone who is in Christ qualifies for heaven.

Can you see it? The test of the judgment is not whether we are worthy *in ourselves*. Rather, it is whether we have faith in Christ. We choose a favorable verdict in the judgment by identifying ourselves with Christ's act of justification.

You understand, I'm sure, that this is not some cheap, second-rate gospel that permits all kinds of monkey business under the guise of faith. True Bible faith requires wholehearted commitment to Christ—commitment that exchanges what the world offers for what Christ offers.

But why even have a judgment at all if God already knows the ones who believe in Him? This brings us to the theme of the great controversy between good and evil.

Satan, father of lies, long ago raised doubts about God's fairness and integrity. He repeated these charges during Christ's

22

days on earth: "This man receiveth sinners" (Luke 15:2). In other words: "How can the Holy One accept the unholy? And if He can forgive sinners, why cast me and my angels out of heaven while building mansions for fallen humanity?"

A number of texts show that celestial beings are intensely interested in questions concerning our salvation.[6] God cannot simply brush aside the devil's accusations. Since His government operates through the loving trust and loyalty of the universe, He must settle doubts about His trustworthiness. So God allows Himself to be audited, so to speak: "Let God be true, but every man a liar; as it is written, That thou mightest be justified in thy sayings, and mightest overcome when thou art judged" (Rom. 3:4).

A Record of Forgiveness

One more thing about the judgment. Sometimes people feel bad about having sins recorded in the sanctuary. But actually, as long as we remain in Christ our sins are forgiven—guilt is gone! So it's not a record of our sins God is keeping up there—it's the record of His forgiveness. His mercy in our lives.

This, then, is what judgment ought to mean for sincere believers. God is on our side, defending our salvation.

You may be thinking, *I really want this assurance. But how far does it go?* Well, it certainly isn't "once saved, always saved." Absolutely not. The devil himself lost his position in heaven by rebelling against God. If we choose to revert to the devil's fallen lifestyle, we will also get ourselves cast out of our heavenly position in Christ.

But if we are willing to reaffirm our repentance daily by keeping alive our faith in Jesus Christ, we can rejoice in the assurance that we are already citizens of the kingdom, sitting in heavenly places with Christ.

You may wonder, though, about the close of probation—where will our hope of salvation be then? Remember the Old Testament time of trouble with the plagues before the exodus to the Promised Land? "The blood shall be a sign for you," God said. "When I see the blood, I will pass over you" (Ex. 12:13).

The blood of Jesus! That's where our hope is—never in our character attainments. When Christ comes in the clouds and the

23

awesome question goes forth "Who shall be able to stand?" His comforting answer will be: "My grace is sufficient for you."

I can't begin to tell you what peace with God through the blood of Christ means to me. Now I really want Jesus to come—and the sooner the better!

---

[1] Isidore Singer, ed., *The Jewish Encyclopedia* (New York: Funk and Wagnalls, 1904), Vol. II, p. 293.

[2] W. M. Chandler, *The Trial of Jesus* (New York: Empire Pub. Co., 1908), vol. 1, pp. 153, 154.

[3] See Taylor Bunch, *Behold the Man!* (Nashville: Southern Pub. Assn., 1940), pp. 64, 66. Now we understand why David in the Psalms longed to be sentenced by divine judgment. See Ps. 35:24.

[4] *Jewish Encyclopedia,* Vol. II, p. 294.

[5] *Jewish Encyclopedia,* Vol. X, p. 204. The Father gave Jesus "authority to exercise judgment also, because He is the Son of Man" (John 5:27, NKJV). Both Father and Son work together to defend us, so both are considered our judges (cf. Heb. 12:23, 24 with Acts 10:40-42). *Both* are also called Saviour (Titus 1:3, 4) and Creator (cf. Mark 13:19 with John 1:3). All three members of the Godhead work in concert.

[6] Consider such texts as 1 Peter 1:12; Eph. 3:10; 1 Cor. 4:9; Ex. 25:20.

Currently associate editor of *Ministry* magazine, Martin Weber has been a literature evangelist, pastor, and author. Before coming to *Ministry,* he served at the Adventist Media Center in California as ministry growth director for the Voice of Prophecy and prayer ministries director for It Is Written. The father of two teenage children, he has authored five books, including *Adventist Hot Potatoes* and *My Tortured Conscience.*

 *The Sabbath*

*T*he beneficent Creator, after the six days of Creation, rested on the seventh day and instituted the Sabbath for all people as a memorial of Creation. The fourth commandment of God's unchangeable law requires the observance of this seventh-day Sabbath as the day of rest, worship, and ministry in harmony with the teaching and practice of Jesus, the Lord of the Sabbath. The Sabbath is a day of delightful communion with God and one another. It is a symbol of our redemption in Christ, a sign of our sanctification, a token of our allegiance, and a foretaste of our eternal future in God's kingdom. The Sabbath is God's perpetual sign of His eternal covenant between Him and His people. Joyful observance of this holy time from evening to evening, sunset to sunset, is a celebration of God's creative and redemptive acts. (Gen. 2:1-3; Ex. 20:8-11; Luke 4:16; Isa. 56:5, 6; 58:13, 14; Matt. 12:1-12; Ex. 31:13-17; Eze. 20:12, 20; Deut. 5:12-15; Heb. 4:1-11; Lev. 23:32; Mark 1:32.)—Fundamental Beliefs, *No. 19.*

CHAPTER THREE

By Charles E. Bradford

The Sabbath and Liberation
With the Sabbath, No One Can Keep Us Down.

T he idea of Sabbath is from the beginning a statement about God's purpose for humanity. It is inextricably bound up with freedom and liberty.

Cain Hope Felder, professor of religion at Howard University, makes this insightful observation: "The seventh day marks a time of completion and Sabbath rest. In a sense, one can find here all the elements that make for the *Shalom* [peace] of God: the goodness of the created order is established; the heavens and the earth are completed; the progenitors of the human family are free to develop their potentials without predetermined restraints. God is at peace with creation, and divine rest is most appropriate." [1]

First Great Freedom Movement

When Israel was in bondage, the Egyptian taskmasters made it virtually impossible for them to observe Sabbath rest. "Pharoah said, 'Lazy, that's what you are—lazy! That is why you keep saying, "Let us go and sacrifice to the Lord." Now get to work. You will not be given any straw, yet you must produce your full quota of bricks.' The Israelite foreman realized they were in trouble" (Ex. 5:17-19).* Under these circumstances, it was virtually impossible for the Hebrews to observe Sabbath rest. Pharaoh refused to grant them the privilege of worship, and even increased their production quotas. They were in danger of losing their identity, their covenant relationship with God.

It was then that Moses delivered the word to Pharaoh: "The Lord, the God of the Hebrews, has sent me to say to you: 'Let my

27

people go, so they may worship me' " (Ex. 7:16). This was an appeal to Pharaoh to allow the people to observe the Sabbath rest.

And evidently the king understood its meaning: "Behold, the people of the land are now many," Pharaoh had said earlier to Moses and Aaron, "and you make them rest from their burdens" (Ex. 5:5, RSV).

So it would seem clear that the Sabbath lay at the very heart of the first great freedom movement. And when the Exodus became an accomplished fact, Yahweh established His Sabbath among His people as a sign of their liberation. "Remember that you were slaves in Egypt and that the Lord your God brought you out of there with a mighty hand and an outstretched arm. Therefore the Lord your God has commanded you to observe the Sabbath day" (Deut. 5:15).

This was not simply to be a temporary arrangement. Sabbath rest and Sabbath observance have something to do with human dignity and freedom. Yahweh never intended for one human being to tyrannize another, or for one nation to subjugate another nation. The Sabbath reminds both master and servant that the Creator-God is the landlord of ultimate concern, who has "made of one blood all nations of men for to dwell on all the face of the earth" (Acts 17:26, KJV).

Reminder of Relationship

We, therefore, are stewards and not proprietors. The creature must be careful not to supersede the prerogatives of the Creator—careful not to usurp His rights. The Sabbath is a sign in perpetuity and a constant reminder of the relationships that exist between human beings and their God and between human beings and their fellow humans—their brothers and sisters.

It will bear repeating. In the Exodus experience God is making a powerful statement for all time about His will for all people, all human beings. And God saw to it that this was recorded for our learning and understanding. And He wants this record to be accessible to His earthborn children so that they might have hope. "I am the Lord your God, who brought you out of Egypt so that you would no longer be slaves to the Egyptians; I broke the bars of your yoke and enabled you to walk with heads held high" (Lev. 26:13).

This is good and exciting news, especially for the oppressed and downtrodden. The Sabbath gives them identity, self-worth, meaning. By observing the Sabbath day they become joined to the liberating God in a special covenant relationship. And He recognizes them as sons and daughters.

"This is what the Lord says: 'Maintain justice and do what is right, for my salvation is close at hand and my righteousness will soon be revealed. Blessed is the man who does this, the man who holds it fast, who keeps the Sabbath without desecrating it, and keeps his hand from doing any evil.' Let no foreigner who has bound himself to the Lord say, 'The Lord will surely exclude me from his people.' And let not any eunuch complain, 'I am only a dry tree.'

"For this is what the Lord says: 'To the eunuchs who keep my Sabbaths, who choose what pleases me and hold fast to my covenant—to them I will give within my temple and its walls a memorial and a name better than sons and daughters; I will give them an everlasting name that will not be cut off.

" 'And foreigners who bind themselves to the Lord to serve him, to love the name of the Lord, and to worship him, all who keep the Sabbath without desecrating it and who hold fast to my covenant— these I will bring to my holy mountain and give them joy in my house of prayer' " (Isa. 56:1-7).

Manifests for All People
This is Yahweh's manifesto for all people who are outside of Israel according to the flesh. What an amazing declaration. How sweeping in its implications. Yahweh commands justice and right doing, especially in the day when His judgments are at hand. His sign of freedom is not restricted to any particular time of earth's history, nor to any people. Old Testament times, New Testament times, foreigners, eunuchs (powerless people—politically and economically impotent), are included. No person on Planet Earth is to be shut out from the covenant relationship and blessings. All may become a part of Israel's history and heritage. "If you belong to Christ, then you are Abraham's seed, and heirs according to the promise" (Gal. 3:29).

Everything that God said about His people Israel and the first

29

great freedom movement—the Exodus—applies to those who take hold of the Sabbath to keep it. They become incorporated into the special people of God, a part of their history. Yahweh gives them all the rights and privileges of true sons and daughters. He promises them freedom and liberation so that they may come out of oppression and worship Him without restriction.

What we are talking about is relevant and applicable to the whole human family, but especially to the outcasts—the poor, the powerless. Yahweh God invites them to His feast and promises to gather them from every part of the earth. (See Isa. 56:8.)

It is no wonder, then, that theologians and biblical scholars in the so-called Third World have taken up this theme of liberation. They have looked at the account of God's great deliverance in the Exodus and are tremendously impressed with the power that He displayed in bringing His people out of bondage.

African-American and Third World theologians feel it their duty to focus on liberation. This is understandable. They are closer to those parts of the world where the misery index is highest. Traditional theology, they say, is done in ivory towers by those who are identified with the "haves." They tell us that God is on the side of the poor and send out a ringing call for justice and equity. They challenge the highly industrialized nations and the religious establishment in these nations to identify with the poor and to "get on God's side."

One hears expressions such as "Liberation—whatever it takes and by whatever means." The suggestion is that even violence is in order. Conservative Bible scholars are looked upon as being accommodationists. Many who have espoused liberation theology now call for secular, political solutions to human problems. And a few have declared themselves radicals.

But I will contend that liberation theology, though some may look upon it as radical, is not really radical enough. The word "radical" means to get at the root of a matter. Political solutions are not the final end. They cannot possibly get to the root of the human dilemma—sin, rebellion against God. Political revolutions only throw out one group of robbers to be succeeded by another gang.

There is, however, an authentic theology of liberation. Jesus

30

came preaching this radical message: "The Spirit of the Sovereign Lord is on me, because the Lord has anointed me to preach good news to the poor. He has sent me to bind up the brokenhearted, to proclaim freedom for the captives and release from darkness for the prisoners, to proclaim the year of the Lord's favor and the day of vengeance of our God, to comfort all who mourn" (Isa. 61:1, 2).

Jesus promises freedom to the nations—total freedom. His message is both radical and revolutionary. His message makes the Sabbath the sign of liberation and independence.

Sign of Freedom

A few years ago a group of Black clergymen in Atlanta, Georgia, expressed their concern about conditions in the American Black church. They spoke courageously about "poverty of soul and spirit." "We do not believe," they said, "that better jobs and bigger houses, color televisions and the latest model cars, prove that people have attained the abundant life of which Jesus spoke. The abundant life cannot be experienced by a people captive to the idolatry of a sin-sick and materialistic culture." [2]

The clergymen spoke about captivity to materialism and went on to repudiate physical gratification as the purpose of life. The great deceiver is busily at work inflaming human passion by one means or another. He enslaves humanity through chemical dependencies, extreme selfishness, insensitivity to the plight of the unfortunate. He plays the part of the pied piper—bewitching, charming, leading the inhabitants of earth toward the point of no return. "The whole world appears to be in the march to death." [3]

We cannot overemphasize the importance of the Sabbath, God's sign of independence and liberty. The powerful God who delivered the Israelites speaks to all of us today who struggle against the overwhelming influences of evil and soul oppression. "Therefore I led them out of Egypt and brought them into the desert. I gave them my decrees and made known to them my laws, for the man who obeys them will live by them. Also I gave them my Sabbaths as a sign between us, so they would know that I the Lord made them holy. . . . Keep my Sabbaths holy, that they may be a sign between us. Then you will know that I am the Lord your God" (Eze. 20:10-20).

Only God can break the spell of slavery and oppression. Only the truth that comes through Jesus—the supreme reality—can liberate us. "Then you will know the truth," Jesus said, "and the truth will set you free" (John 8:32).

It is time for all people to make God's sign of liberation their banner. "In that day the Root of Jesse will stand as a banner for the peoples; the nations will rally to him, and his place of rest will be glorious. In that day the Lord will reach out his hand a second time to reclaim the remnant that is left of his people from Assyria, from Lower Egypt, from Upper Egypt, from Cush, from Elam, from Babylonia, from Hamath, and from the islands of the sea. He will raise a banner for the nations and gather the exiles of Israel; he will assemble the scattered people of Judah from the four quarters of the earth" (Isa. 11:10-12).

We must now look to the end of the biblical history of Israel as well as to the beginning. Even James Cone, a leading exponent of liberation theology, admits that "the struggle for justice in this world is not the ultimate goal of faith." Yahweh God has made His statement. He is for freedom, liberty, dignity, and for the empowerment of all people. "And afterward, I will pour out my Spirit on all people. Your sons and daughters will prophesy, your old men will dream dreams, your young men will see visions. Even on my servants, both men and women, I will pour out my Spirit in those days" (Joel 2:28, 29).

God is for the poor in a special sense, but He invites the rich also to His banquet. The most radical concept of all is articulated in John's victory shout: "The kingdom of the world has become the kingdom of our Lord and of his Christ, and he will reign for ever and ever" (Rev. 11:15). And in that kingdom there will be no oppression. The lion and the lamb will lie down together. Children will play without fear of harm and danger. The destroyer will be put out of business, and the earth itself, long ravaged by sin, will enjoy its Sabbath rest.

Then the promise to the people who have taken hold of God and His covenant will become a constant for all eternity. " 'From one New Moon to another and from one Sabbath to another, all mankind will come and bow down before me,' says the Lord" (Isa. 66:23).

THE SABBATH AND LIBERATION

* Unless otherwise noted, Scripture references in this chapter are from the New International Version.

[1] Cain Hope Felder, *Troubling Biblical Waters* (Orbis), p. 168.
[2] *Christian Spirituality* (Crossroads), vol. 3, p. 401.
[3] *Evangelism,* p. 26.

Retired former president of the North American Division of the General Conference, Charles E. Bradford has had a long and distinguished career in the church. He has served as pastor, regional conference president, associate secretary in the General Conference, and member and president of numerous institutional governing boards. Widely recognized among his peers as a scholar, he has taught and lectured, and wrote the fourth quarter 1984 adult Sabbath School lesson quarterly, as well as the accompanying lesson help book.

Death and Resurrection

*T*he wages of sin is death. But God, who alone is immortal, will grant eternal life to His redeemed. Until that day death is an unconscious state for all people. When Christ, who is our life, appears, the resurrected righteous and the living righteous will be glorified and caught up to meet their Lord. The second resurrection, the resurrection of the unrighteous, will take place a thousand years later. (Rom. 6:23; 1 Tim. 6:15, 16; Eccl. 9:5, 6; Ps. 146:3, 4; John 11:11-14; Col. 3:4; 1 Cor. 15:51-54; 1 Thess. 4:13-17; John 5:28, 29; Rev. 20:1-10.)—Fundamental Beliefs, *No. 25.*

CHAPTER FOUR

By Ronald Alan Knott

Immortality or Resurrection?
How Adventist Faith Brings Hope

Every air-traveling Adventist has at least one story about witnessing on the wing. Here's mine.

It was December 30, the next to the last day of the year. I was returning home to Andrews University after spending the Christmas holiday with friends. I found a window seat and settled in.

A moment later another passenger came to my row and took her place on the aisle, leaving an empty seat between us. She was in her mid-30s, sharply dressed in casual clothes, thin, with precisely styled, short-cropped red hair. I was in high mood, and ready to chitchat with anybody.

"And where are you headed?"

She was friendly and willing to talk. Her soft voice flowed gently with the easy grace of an apparently affluent Southern heritage. This was later confirmed by her unpretentious revelation that her grandfather had been a governor of Texas. Somewhere among the details I got the impression that she had some typical Southern Protestant background—perhaps Southern Baptist or Methodist. But the fact that she worked in Washington, D.C., as a lobbyist for an educational association prompted me to the perhaps prejudicial thought that conventional religion might no longer play a large part in her life.

Today she was flying back to Washington, cutting her Christmas holiday short to attend the funeral of a close friend. The services would be the next day, December 31.

"In a strange sort of way I'm looking forward to that funeral,"

35

she said wistfully. "It seems sort of fitting that it will be on the last day of the year."

"Why is that?"

"I guess I'm hoping it will help me put a final end to this terrible year and leave it all behind me."

In the next few minutes I heard the wrenching story of how five of this gentle woman's close relatives, friends, and work associates had died during that calendar year, all from some form of cancer. And one of the five was her father.

It began to dawn on me that I might have something to offer to this hurting person. The moral of every inspiring witnessing story I had ever heard seemed to thunder in my head: that God had put me on this flight to speak for Him now. In short, I felt commanded to share my faith.

How to Help?

But how? I knew nothing about the techniques of comforting the grieving. In fact, funerals and their related traumas and customs have always been doubly difficult occasions for me. First, I must face my own sadness and loss. But then I am caught in the sometimes immense social awkwardness of wanting to comfort the most grieving ones and yet fearing I will say something stupid. Expressing sympathy and deep feelings never has been my strong point.

She paused in her story. I could think of nothing better than "I'm sorry." Was that all I was going to be able to offer?

She sighed and then said softly, "I just can't believe that God is going to make them all burn in hell forever. That just doesn't seem fair. How can that be love?"

In those few words she had solved my witnessing dilemma, or so I thought. She had rescued me from the murky world of "feeling" and turned the conversation to Christian doctrine—something specific and objective. I could deal with that.

I answered quickly, confident for the moment that I could handle this. "I don't believe that they are burning in hell now, or that they will burn forever," I said smoothly. "That's because I believe the Bible doesn't teach that our souls live on forever, or that we go to heaven or hell when we die, or that God will make people suffer conscious torment forever."

I caught my breath, eager to forge ahead. But in a horrible second it dawned on me that I had very little more to say.

She waited, her gaze obviously expecting some evidence for my bold and hopeful claim. And in that terrible moment I realized I had no evidence to give—not because I doubted in the least that my claim was true or that the evidence was there, but simply because, despite 26 years of Adventism, I had never bothered to learn it for sharing with someone else.

My mind whirled. Perhaps this woman knew her Bible. Perhaps she knew it better than I did. If so, any evidence I offered must come clearly and directly *from the Bible*. That meant texts. But what were all those texts I should use? I panicked. Something in Ecclesiastes came to mind, but then everything went blank.

End of Conversation

I thought about the small Bible I carried in the camera bag stowed correctly under the seat in front of me. My better judgment shouted not to touch it. It seemed wiser in this horrible mess to make some flat, textless assertions and leave her guessing me an absolute simpleton than to engage in a fruitless forage through Scripture and remove all possible doubt. Numbed by my stunning failure to do what I felt called to do, I reached for the flight magazine and ended the conversation.

That experience has haunted me ever since. Did I fail, or had I done my appointed work? Either through grace or rationalization, I have come to believe that I may have accomplished God's purpose after all. Perhaps my simple—or simplistic—assertions had planted the seed of hope in that woman's heart that God would cultivate in His own way. At the same time, that incident also judged me for the evidence of my faith, at least on one point, and found me very wanting.

That sad woman I met on the plane represents millions in our society—Christians and non-Christians—who long for concrete answers about what happens when we die. For some, like this woman, it is a longing born of immediate and almost unbearable grief. For others it is just the curiosity to know the unknowable.

The entertainment industry and the popular press pander to

the public fascination. Hollywood makes millions on movies like *Ghost,* assuming an immediate afterlife. The March 1992 issue of *Life* magazine devoted its lengthy cover story to the questions raised by "near-death experiences" (NDE)—reports of warm and fuzzy out-of-body experiences by people who were resuscitated after showing few signs of life. According to the article, interest has boomed in NDEs since the 1975 publication of *Life After Life,* by Raymond Moody. A compilation of NDE anecdotes, the book has sold 7 million copies and sparked, even in the scientific community, an "open discussion of these visions [that] has begun to change the climate of dying in America." [1]

Popular View

If the climate of dying has changed, the beliefs surrounding it have not; for the article further notes that the "popular view of near-death experiences is based largely on a view of existence that has scarcely changed in millennia: the belief that the body is inhabited by a soul or spirit or mind that informs our consciousness and leaves the body at death." [2]

Virtually alone among organized Christian denominations, world religions, or modern mysticisms and spiritualisms (like the New Age), Seventh-day Adventists stand firmly and surprisingly united against this view. This puts us at odds and risks our popularity with virtually everybody except hard-core atheists. Some among us, sadly, may argue over the nature of Jesus, the meaning of His death, or the validity of a pre-Advent judgment. But I have yet to meet an Adventist who is even remotely squishy on the nonimmortality of the soul.

Why is this? It is not that those other doctrines are any less "provable" from Scripture. They may be even more so. It is more likely that our understanding of the state of the dead makes such perfect sense, that it is so foundational to everything else we know about the character of God, the nature of sin, and the great controversy between our Saviour Jesus Christ and Satan—that great deceiver, the one who, "when he lies, . . . speaks his native language" (John 8:44, NIV).

In Eden our Creator said plainly to Adam and Eve that if they disobeyed Him (sinned) by eating of the tree in the middle of the

garden, they would "surely die." That simple declaration ought to
be biblical evidence enough that God did not give us immortal
souls capable of relating to Him outside of physical life. Yet in case
we missed the point, text after text throughout Scripture affirms
this.

Psalm 6:5 says: "No one remembers you when he is dead. Who
praises you from the grave?" (NIV). Psalm 115:17 says: "It is not
the dead who praise the Lord, those who go down to silence" (NIV).
And of course, there is the classic statement in Ecclesiastes 9:5, 6:
"For the living know that they will die, but the dead know nothing;
. . . Their love, their hate and their jealousy have long since
vanished; never again will they have a part in anything that
happens under the sun" (NIV).[3]

Our understanding of the nonimmortality of the soul addresses
and dispenses with the first and most fundamental lie of Satan in
Eden, when he told Eve, "You will not surely die." To Adolf Hitler
has been attributed the claim that it is easier to make people
believe a big lie than a little one. Sadly, on this vital matter of
what happens when we die, virtually the entire world, including
Christendom, has confirmed the validity of Hitler's horrible prov-
erb.

Once having believed that first big lie, humanity has inevita-
bly committed itself to accepting a broad selection of other lies that
come with it. Some of them are mutually exclusive but equally
enticing to the mind of any age, particularly to ours. In all the
recent interest in near-death experiences, has anyone yet received
a hint of hell or punishment of evil? No. It's nothing but sweetness
and light. The obvious message the deceiver would have us believe
is that everyone, regardless of life or faith, will, upon death, ascend
to some nebulous but glorious reward. Thus, if there is no punishment for sin, there must, in effect, be no such thing as sin.

Making God a Sadist

Apparently contradicting this lie, but equally deceptive, is the
doctrine of an eternally burning hell. God said that sin means
death. That rules out any eternal lake of fire in which sinners are
kept alive forever in punishment. But most of Christendom has
accepted the idea of eternal torment. This idea also is rooted

squarely in Satan's first lie, "You will not surely die." If we, unlike NDE adherents, correctly believe that sin will be punished, then a concurrent belief in an immortal soul eventually forces us to conclude that God is nothing more than a cosmic monster. How could a truly just and loving God repay a mere 70 or 80 years of sinful living on earth with endless, eternal ages of unspeakably excruciating conscious torment? God becomes a tyrant we must fear and cannot love. That, of course, was the unspoken conclusion of my friend on the plane.

After these falsehoods comes spiritualism. This has the potential to be the most sinister, and in its varied forms is becoming more popular all the time. Through supposed revelations from those who've gone before, the credulous become easy victims of all manner of new deceptions.

Our doctrine of the nonimmortality of the soul, perhaps more than any other, sets us apart from the rest of organized religion in a way that can grab the attention of the masses. It puts all faith in the context of the great controversy. It declares that God is our Creator, that disobedience is the cause of all our woe. It proclaims a God of love who hates sin and yet is merciful and just in His final judgment of it. It meets the uncertainty and fear of a hurting world around us and points them to a loving, soon-returning Saviour who will call His children to a new, resurrected life in Him.

Are We Willing—And Able?

This doctrine will do all those things, but only if we are willing and able to share it. In my conversation with the woman on the plane, I clearly was *willing* to share it. But even more clearly I was *not able* to share it. I knew the destination, but I could not point the way. How many of my under-40 peers in Adventism would be different? Not many, I'm afraid.

In my elementary school days, just before the age of calculators, my arithmetic teachers labored with me over long division. They were interested not only in the correct answer, but in the process by which I got it. And a few years later, in chemistry and physics, my teachers were actually *more* interested in the process of my calculations than the product.

Of course, I realize my salvation has more to do with responding to a simple understanding of God's character as revealed through His Son than with knowing the nuts and bolts of how I arrived at that view. It's more important for me to know, deep in my being, that God is love than it is to know, deep in my brain, that a certain text says so. But that doesn't help anyone but me. How can my convictions help anyone else if I can't give him or her specific, credible evidences from some authority outside myself?

Perhaps more than any doctrine, Adventist understanding of the nonimmortality of the soul will find practical use meeting with the man and woman on the street and sharing our faith. But we've got to have something to say. For me, this means some serious Bible study, and yes, even some good old-fashioned memorization.

Six years after my encounter with that woman on the plane, I was making another cross-country trip. The long flight gave me a good chance to do some background reading in preparation for writing this article. Somewhere over Ohio, while browsing through the relevant sections of *Questions on Doctrine,* I glanced at the man in the seat across the aisle. He was reading a book. The title was *Death and the After-Life.*

"And where are you headed?"

---

[1] Verlyn Klinkenborg, "At the Edge of Eternity," *Life,* Mar. 1992, p. 66.
[2] *Ibid.,* p. 73.
[3] See also Ps. 30:9; 88:10; 146:4; Isa. 38:18; and 1 Cor. 15:17, 18.

Ronald Alan Knott is a graduate of Atlantic Union College and worked for nine years in public relations at Andrews University before joining the General Conference staff in 1990. He is currently invalved in a special project for the General Conference, producing a video documentary on Millerism. He is married to Esther Ramharacksingh Knott, associate pastor of the Sligo SDA Church.

The Holy Scriptures

*T*he Holy Scriptures, Old and New Testaments, are the written Word of God, given by divine inspiration through holy men of God who spoke and wrote as they were moved by the Holy Spirit. In this Word, God has committed to man the knowledge necessary for salvation. The Holy Scriptures are the infallible revelation of His will. They are the standard of character, the test of experience, the authoritative revealer of doctrines, and the trustworthy record of God's acts in history. (2 Peter 1:20, 21; 2 Tim. 3:16, 17; Ps. 119:105; Prov. 30:5, 6; Isa. 8:20; John 17:17; 1 Thess. 2:13; Heb. 4:12.)—
Fundamental Beliefs, *No. 1.*

CHAPTER FIVE

By Alden Thompson

Adventists and the Bible
Our Heritage and Our Challenge

Adventists are people of the Book. A touch of history can help us remember why. Our modern world challenges us to find new ways to implement the how.

The Bible Unchained

In July of 1546 a royal decree went forth from England's King Henry VIII: "No man or woman of what estate, condition, or degree," was, after the last day of August, to "receive, have, take, or keep Tyndale's or Coverdale's New Testament." With tears the king had addressed a weeping Parliament, complaining that the book was "disputed, rhymed, sung, and jangled in every alehouse and tavern." [1]

Tears of a different kind came from more ordinary folk. The flyleaf of a secular book, Polydore Vergil's *History of Inventions*, has preserved a plaintive handwritten note: "When I kepe Mr. Letymers shepe I bout thys boke when the Testament was oberragated, that shepherds myght not rede hit. I pray God amende that blindness. Wryt by Robert Wyllyams, keppying shepe upon Seynburyhill, 1546."

Yes, the Bible elicits strong passions from human hearts. The quotations from King Henry and Shepherd Wyllyams throw into bold relief the contrasting perspectives that battled for supremacy at the time of the Reformation: some were seeking to protect the Bible; others were eager to share. For centuries the church carefully shielded the sacred text of Scripture from the longing eyes and gnarled hands of the common people. God spoke Latin, but the people spoke English. How could they hear His Word?

John Wycliffe vowed to change all that. Some 150 years before Henry VIII, Wycliffe unchained the Bible, put it into English, and gave it back to the people. "No man is so rude a scholar," said Wycliffe, "but that he might learn the words of the gospel according to his simplicity." Whether clergy, knight, or commoner, "it helpeth Christian men to study the gospel in that tongue in which they know best Christ's sentence."

Since there were no printing presses yet, copies of Wycliffe's English Bible were expensive. But the Word went out, and the people rejoiced.

The authorities, however, were not pleased. The Oxford Council of 1407 prohibited both the translation and the reading of any book of Scripture "composed in the time of the said John Wycliffe or later." Yet hungry souls were eager to circumvent the ban. At least one Bible has been preserved from that era carrying an original date of MCCCCVIII (1408) but with one "C" erased, yielding a date of 1308 and, presumably, exemption from the ban.

The first printed New Testament was the work of John Tyndale. But it was dangerous business. Tyndale was hunted down on the continent and burned at the stake. A similar fate awaited others. Someone has noted that of all the early English Reformation translators, only Miles Coverdale died in bed.

Our Heritage

In our world, Robert Wyllyams, the shepherd of Seynburyhill, would likely implore the Lord to "amende" a different kind of blindness. While the thirst for God's Word is intense in places newly liberated from autocratic rule, the lands that gave birth to the Reformation have gone back to sleep. Could it be that restoring the Bible to its proper place is another special task God has given to the remnant of the woman's seed? For us, Tyndale's reasons for daring to put God's Word into the hands of the people are worth pondering. "I had perceived by experience," he said, "how that it was impossible to establish the laypeople in any truth, except the Scripture were plainly laid before their eyes in their mother tongue, that they might see the process, order, and meaning of the text."

Our spiritual forebears proclaimed Advent and Sabbath to a

44

Christian world that had largely forgotten both. In our day—at least in America—the Advent hope fares better than the Sabbath. But now the Bible itself, the very source that teaches us the Adventist hope and the Sabbath truth, is suffering from neglect.

That neglect presents Adventists with a special challenge and an opportunity. Our Adventist heritage reminds us that we have good reason to revere God's Word. Our founders flew in the face of popular opinion when they preached the Second Advent. They ran counter to popular practice when they preached the Sabbath. But they did it because the Bible says so.

The Only Standard

Consistently in our statements of beliefs we have claimed the Bible as our only standard. The unofficial statement of 1872 affirms that "we have no articles of faith, creed, or discipline aside from the Bible"; it is "the only infallible rule of faith and practice." The first official statement in 1931 called the Bible "the only unerring rule of faith and practice." Finally, in 1980, in the first formal statement of beliefs to be fully discussed and voted at a General Conference in session, the very first words read: "Seventh-day Adventists accept the Bible as their only creed."

The role of the Bible in Adventism is even more striking in today's world because of the emphasis we have given to an *intelligent* use of the Bible. As Ellen White put it: "The truths of the divine Word can be best appreciated by an intellectual Christian. Christ can be best glorified by those who serve Him intelligently." [2]

To serve God intelligently means we exhibit a certain healthy skepticism when we listen to other people interpret the Bible, whether they are scholars, preachers, or church leaders. Again, in the words of Ellen White: "We are not to accept the opinion of commentators as the voice of God; they were erring mortals like ourselves. God has given reasoning powers to us as well as to them." [3] "Those who have not been in the habit of searching the Bible for themselves, or weighing evidence, have confidence in the leading men and accept the decisions they make; and thus many will reject the very messages God sends to His people, if these leading brethren do not accept them." [4]

45

To be sure, intellect alone cannot fully grasp the truths of God's Word. Ellen White warned that the mind can actually be "clouded with doubt" if "the Word of God is opened without reverence and without prayer." [5] In short, Adventists are called to be both intelligent and devout when handling God's Word, a calling that offers us a peculiar opportunity and challenge in our modern world.

The nature of that challenge was highlighted by Nathan Hatch in an address to the presidents of independent colleges in America.[6] Hatch, an evangelical church historian, pointed out the frustrating dilemma facing the church, namely, that where the intellectual element has played a prominent role in the church, as in Europe, the church has been weak. By contrast, where the intellectual element has been weak, as in America, the church seems robust.

The survey statistics cited by Hatch are sobering. In America, for example, in response to a question about the role of religion in their future life, 40 percent of the young people queried said religion would be "very important" to them. In Germany, France, and Britain, however, only 10 percent made that claim; in Scandinavia only 5 percent. One of Hatch's concluding comments was a challenge to the presidents: "College administrators have no greater responsibility than to nurture a new generation of Christian thinkers." [7]

Can Adventists be part of that new generation of Christian thinkers? I believe so. Of course, we will want to do our part in satisfying the intense hunger of God's Word in newly liberated lands. But in attempting to face reality in the "Christian" West, too, we can recognize that the different circumstances in Europe and America illustrate the two quite different challenges facing us. Simply put, in places dominated by secularism (Europe, for example) we must *awaken* interest in Scripture; in places where religion tends to be popular but superficial (America, for example) our task is to *deepen* interest in the Word.

1. *Awakening Interest in Scripture.* If we are to catch the attention of a contented and satisfied secular world, we must show that the Bible produces a faith that makes a difference in the world, both in people's personal lives and in the condition of the earth itself. That means taking Jesus' two great commands seri-

ously as the focus of all our efforts. And I do mean *focus,* for when Jesus said that we must first love God wholeheartedly and then our fellow humans as ourselves, He went on to say that *"all* the Law and the Prophets hang on these two" (Matt. 22:35-40, NIV). Tithing mint, anise, and cummin may be important. But justice, mercy, and faith are indeed *weightier* matters (Matt. 23:23). That must be clear to anyone who sees Adventists in action. In our lives and witness, loving people and establishing justice on earth must stand at the head of our agenda.

2. *Deepening Interest in Scripture.* Increasingly I am convinced that the tendency among Christians to avoid the serious study of Scripture stems from two basic reasons. First, the feeling that much of the Bible is irrelevant to our life. This makes it easier for believers simply to worship God without making Bible study an integral part of the life of faith. Second, the fear of confronting unsettling complexities in Scripture, even apparent contradictions. This makes it easier to defend the Bible than to study.

The Adventist Advantage

I believe our Adventist heritage places us in an excellent position to address both issues effectively and consistently.

A major problem for many devout believers is the failure to take seriously Jesus' statements that *some commands are more important than others*. That doesn't mean we keep only the "important" ones and throw the others away. The more important commands simply provide the framework within which all other commands are to be fulfilled. The tendency of believers to view every sentence of Scripture as being of *equal* and *absolute* value not only makes it difficult to find relevance in some biblical commands but also causes great discomfort when we come face-to-face with commands that we are not prepared to implement.

A good test case is God's command to stone a man for picking up sticks on the Sabbath (Num. 15:32-36). If God gave that command, why don't we obey it today? I doubt if even the staunchest Christian Sabbathkeeper would attempt to obey that law in detail. So let's skip it . . .

No. It's part of Scripture. Let's take it seriously and ask what it means. The only tool available for such a task is our reason. May

47

Ellen White's words ring in our ears: "God has given reasoning powers to us as well as to them." And of course, when we consult reason we must do so in an attitude of prayer. The choice is not between prayer and thinking. What we want is prayerful thinking. The praying Christian will be thinking more, not less.

Our next step is to look at our "problem" passage in the light of Scripture, *all* Scripture. Letting the Bible itself shed light on the Bible is what Protestants have meant by the principle "The Bible is its own best interpreter." The church does not interpret the Bible for us; the believer consults the Bible itself by means of prayerful reason. With reference to the specific command to stone Sabbathbreakers, Scripture itself reveals in both Testaments that the penalty aspect of law was not applied consistently. The New Testament, especially, would lead us to believe that God prefers promises to penalties. But He will use whatever is needed to bring wholehearted love to God and faithful love between people. The Sabbath command endures, even if the death penalty does not apply.

In *Patriarchs and Prophets* Ellen White carefully develops a biblical approach to law, arguing that the **one** *great principle of love* (Rom. 13:8-10) is further defined by the **two** *great commands* (Matt. 22:35-40).[8] But Israel needed more help than that. So God gave the **Ten** *Commandments*. Israel needed still more help. So God gave *even more* specific commands. In the words of Ellen White: "That the obligations of the Decalogue might be more fully understood and enforced, additional precepts were given, illustrating and applying the principles of the Ten Commandments."[9] The most pointed biblical statement in that connection comes in Matthew 19:8, where Jesus declares that God gave the law of divorce because "you were so hard-hearted" (NRSV). Thus we find in Scripture many commands that are conditioned by the time, place, and circumstances of the people to whom God is speaking.

Those time-conditioned commands, however, can still be very helpful in our day, for by illustrating how God has dealt with people in times past, the "cases" guide our decisions today.[10]

Adventists, then, can be faithful to the *one, two,* and *ten* and be consistent. That law pyramid endures throughout Scripture. Like the beams in an A-frame cabin, those pillars remain firmly in place. One can remodel the kitchen if need be, but the house is not at risk. The *one,* the *two,* and the *ten* are there to stay. If we can appreciate how that stable framework protects us from the slippery slope, then we can be more open and honest with the rest of Scripture, practicing justice, mercy, and faith (Matt. 23:23) in all our dealings with all people everywhere.

The Bible is a book for all people everywhere. Adventists are in a marvelous position to show the world that we cherish God's Word and are seeking to make it relevant and applicable to life on earth. We serve a God who has shown us how to live and to love. He's coming back to take us home with Him. What good news we have to share with the world!

---

[1] Historical quotations are from H. Wheeler Robinson, ed., *The Bible in Its Ancient and English Versions* (New York: Oxford University Press, 1940, 1954).

[2] *Testimonies,* vol. 3, p. 160.

[3] *Testimonies to Ministers,* p. 106.

[4] *Ibid.,* pp. 106, 107.

[5] *Testimonies,* vol. 5, pp. 704, 705.

[6] *Private Higher Education: Celebrating Diversity* (Scottsdale, Ariz.: American Association of Presidents of Independent Colleges and Universities, 1988), vol. 16, pp. 2-7.

[7] *Ibid.,* p. 7.

[8] For a more extended development of these thoughts, see the author's *Inspiration: Hard Questions, Honest Answers* (Hagerstown, Md.: Review and Herald Pub. Assn., 1991).

[9] *Patriarchs and Prophets,* p. 310.

[10] For a more extended development of these thoughts, see *Inspiration: Hard Questions, Honest Answers.*

Professor of biblical studies at Walla Walla College, Alden Thompson pastored in California before entering teaching. Born to missionary parents, he spent the first four years of his life in Medellin, Colombia. His special teaching interests are Old Testament and Seventh-day Adventist history. He has written a monthly column in *Signs of the Times* since 1985 and authored *Who's Afraid of the Old Testament God?* and *Inspiration: Hard Questions, Honest Answers.* Dr. Thompson has two daughters.

The Gift of Prophecy

One of the gifts of the Holy Spirit is prophecy. This gift is an identifying mark of the remnant church and was manifested in the ministry of Ellen G. White. As the Lord's messenger, her writings are a continuing and authoritative source of truth which provide for the church comfort, guidance, instruction, and correction. They also make clear that the Bible is the standard by which all teaching and experience must be tested. (Joel 2:28, 29; Acts 2:14-21; Heb. 1:1-3; Rev. 12:17; 19:10.)—Fundamental Beliefs, No. 17.

CHAPTER SIX

By Roy Adams

A Prophet for Our Time
Sizing Up Ellen G. White

In countless sermons and talks over the years, Adventists have recounted the historical drama of Luther's appearance before the Diet of Worms. Facing the assembled dignitaries of church and state, the embattled cleric refused to surrender his allegiance to the Bible. "My conscience is held captive to the Word of God," he insisted in the face of overwhelming pressure to back down. "I cannot, and I will not, recant. Here I stand."

With all Protestants, we have admired this ringing affirmation of the fundamental authority of Scripture. But do we merely pay lip service to "the Bible and the Bible only," falling back on the authority of an extrabiblical source to defend our beliefs and doctrines? Do we proclaim *sola scriptura*[1] out one side of the mouth and from the other superimpose on Scripture the authority of Ellen G. White? What justification do we have for this "peculiar" approach to the concept of *sola scriptura?*

Such questions are not new, of course. But new people are coming into the church all the time. And our own children, moreover, must struggle with this apparent inconsistency as soon as they are old enough to catch on. I write for them in particular— but also to strengthen the conviction of those already established in the faith.

Can We Have It Both Ways?

Do Adventists want to have their cake and eat it too? Are we inconsistent?

No. Every description of spiritual gifts in the New Testament

51

lists the gift of prophecy as one of the *charismata*[2] to exist in the church until the end of time.

One of the clearest statements is Ephesians 4:8-16.* "And his gifts were that some should be apostles, some *prophets,* some evangelists, some pastors and teachers . . . until we all attain to the unity of the faith and of the knowledge of the Son of God, to mature manhood, to the measure of the stature of the fulness of Christ." [3]

In logic that could hardly be improved upon, our pioneers argued that the phenomenon of contemporary prophecy could not, therefore, be dismissed out of hand on the basis of Scripture. On the contrary, Scripture itself provides the warrant for this manifestation in the last days. And here, to Paul's clear affirmations, they added the divine promise in the book of Joel: "And it shall come to pass afterward, that I will pour out my spirit on all flesh; your sons and your daughters shall prophesy, your old men shall dream dreams, and your young men shall see visions" (Joel 2:28, 29).

What all this means, at bottom, is that our acceptance of the phenomenon of the contemporary prophet springs from the more fundamental acceptance of the authority of Scripture. Had Scripture ruled out any possibility of such recurrence after the close of the canon, then there could have been no place in Christian teaching for it. Our openness to the phenomenon, therefore, springs from the openness of Scripture itself to it.

Thus, there is no logical discrepancy between our acceptance of the prophetic office of Ellen G. White and our adherence to the concept of *sola scriptura.*

It's Not Up to Us

But why do we need another prophet when we have the Bible?

The question is a valid one. However, *we* do not decide when *we* need a prophet. God, in His inscrutable wisdom, makes that determination. Therefore, the more important question is not why we need another prophet, but whether, indeed, God has sent one.

My considered judgment is that He has—and for good reason. With many others, I have come to believe that without the unifying presence among us of this gift, manifested through the ministry of Ellen G. White, the Seventh-day Adventist Church, as such, would long since have disintegrated. One can identify many crucial points in our history when the church would almost certainly have floundered, except for the steadying hand of God through the contemporary prophetic gift.

The aftermath of 1844, for example; or, the difficult days surrounding the organization of this movement in 1863; or, the 1888 Minneapolis debate over righteousness by faith; or, the holy flesh/pantheistic crisis at the turn of the century.

The 1888 Minneapolis debate over righteousness by faith pitted the youthful A. T. Jones and E. J. Waggoner against such powerful church leaders as G. I. Butler (the iron-willed president of the General Conference) and Uriah Smith (secretary of the General Conference and editor of the *Review and Herald*).

Tell me, if you were in Ellen G. White's position—unguided by a divine source—which, likely, would have appeared to you as the more comfortable and convenient side to choose? But as it turned out, Mrs. White sided with Jones and Waggoner—mere upstarts in comparison with the seasoned veterans arrayed against them. And a century later, Adventist theologians look back with a huge sigh of relief over the position Mrs. White took.

None of the other crisis points was any less dangerous. Each one contained its own peculiar "land mines." But in every case she steered a course between them, choosing each time the side that looked less attractive—from the standpoint of conservative Adventism. Unschooled in formal theology, she was, nevertheless, able to see through the deceptive theological camouflages that threatened the church.

These are matters of history, and in terms of validating the prophetic role of Mrs. White, I find them enormously persuasive and convincing.

Weathering the Storm

The sustained opposition to the role and message of Mrs. White in the Adventist Church should hardly surprise us. After all, this has been the lot of prophets down through history. Did not Miriam and Aaron—no less—question the special status of Moses as spokesman (prophet) for God (Num. 12:1, 2)? Was not Elijah rejected (1 Kings 18:17)? and Jeremiah (Jer. 20:1, 2; 38:1-6)? and

John the Baptist (John 3:25-30)? And did not Jesus weep over a nation that killed His prophets and stoned His messengers (Matt. 23:29-31, 37)?

Every species of objection has been put forward over the years against the validity of Mrs. White's prophetic calling. See, for example, the ones addressed by F. D. Nichol in his book *Ellen G. White and Her Critics.*[4] But while some objections die with time—like the one based on gender (how silly that sounds now)—others renew themselves with every generation.

Still others seem to have a touch of novelty about them—like the one that claims to accept the writings of Mrs. White in a "pastoral," but not in a "canonical," sense. In other words, hers is to give pastoral exhortation only—to tell us how we should live, how we should pray, and what kind of Christians we ought to be. But when it comes to questions of doctrine and theology, then she must take a back seat to scholars and theologians.

I find this approach theologically illogical and unacceptable. For if we believe that God spoke through her, then obviously God can say anything He wishes through her—whether those things relate to pastoral concerns or to doctrinal or theological questions. The distinction here between "canonical" and "pastoral" is artificial and contrived, and represents an arbitrary dichotomy, designed mischievously to divert attention from the main issue: whether God spoke through Mrs. White or not. It would leave each person free to set aside her views whenever they prove inconvenient or embarrassing.

And did she borrow from other writers? That's another question people ask. The underlying assumption here is that the inspired writer receives the message from the Lord word for word, and that every idea expressed by the prophet must be original, never having been expressed before.

These are false assumptions, and those who hold to them must eventually repudiate not only the writings of Ellen G. White, but the Bible itself. Unlike many fundamentalist Christians, Adventists do not believe in verbal inspiration. We do not believe that the Holy Spirit dictated the actual words the prophet was to use. The thoughts, the ideas, the visions, come from the Spirit. But the words used in expressing those thoughts are the prophet's own. Ellen White herself made this crystal clear in many places.[5]

Although it's received more widespread attention in recent years, the fact that Ellen G. White borrowed has been public information for more than 100 years. As early as 1888 the introduction to *The Great Controversy* carried a statement to this effect.[6]

As many readers well know, the use of previously existing sources is a phenomenon of Scripture itself. The writer of the Chronicles testifies that a whole catalog of canonical and noncanonical reference materials was available to him, and again and again refers his readers to them.[7] And Luke indicates clearly that in writing his Gospel he made use of sources (Luke 1:1-4).

When I attended seminary in the late sixties, debate raged in the scholarly world as to which of the Synoptic Gospels borrowed from which. The common view suggested that Mark was first, and that both Luke and Matthew borrowed from it as well as from a (mysterious) source identified as "Q."

And many doubted that the Gospels were, in fact, authentic portrayals of the life of Christ, seeing them rather as theological concoctions of the early church. The entire New Testament was subjected to the most thoroughgoing scrutiny, and all kinds of parallels between it and noncanonical sources were "discovered."

Today the bankruptcy of that kind of scholarship has been exposed—whether in reference to the New Testament or the writings of Mrs. White.

Ellen White was apparently not God's first choice—Hazen Foss, for example, decidedly refused the prophetic call. Perhaps others were more talented or better suited for the work than she. She was, after all, only 17 years of age, sickly, with only a third-grade education. But in spite of these limitations, God chose her—"the weakest of the weak," as she sometimes described herself—and demonstrated His power through her.

In her eagerness for spiritual things, she read widely—her personal library contained some 700 volumes at peak (an unusual accomplishment for her time). It was God who led her and gave her strength to apply herself. God gave her visions and dreams,

55

bringing numerous scenes in the history of the great controversy before her mind.

These often came in the form of flashes, impressions, pictures. The actual words were not supplied. Like all the ancient prophets, she had to find the words to describe what she had seen. Thus, selectively, she'd sometimes utilize the words and descriptions of others, where appropriate.

But if anyone imagines he or she could simply borrow from a few authors and produce a *Desire of Ages,* for example, let them try it. There is a depth and power there that cannot be explained. Which reminds me of the Sermon on the Mount. Some have noted, perhaps with a touch of exaggeration, that every major utterance of the Sermon on the Mount had already been given by someone else. Nevertheless, the power of that sermon has continued unabated after 2,000 years.

I read somewhere that during the First World War the Society of Friends printed the Sermon on the Mount as a separate pamphlet, without comment, for distribution among the allied forces. Both the British and French governments banned it and forbade its circulation among their troops on grounds that it was subversive of national policy.[8] What power—after 20 long centuries! How can we explain it? In the light of such living power, the charge of borrowing stands out as infantile, picayune.

Not Gullible—Thankful!

As our past history makes abundantly clear to anyone who takes the time to study it, Adventists have not been gullible. We accepted the messages of Ellen White as valid only after the most excruciating and painstaking process any prophetic candidate would care to undergo. But eventually we embraced them, and the church has been the better for it.

If God in His mercy has seen fit, pursuant to our own salvation, to give us this precious gift, let us be grateful for it. Whenever I see Adventists mindlessly casting aspersion on this endowment, I am reminded of those powerful words of Shakespeare, put into the mouth of King Lear after two of his daughters, to whom he had bequeathed all his fortune, abandoned him to the cold and tempest.

"How sharper than a serpent's tooth it is," he said, "to have a thankless child." [9]

Let's not insult the Lord by our ingratitude for this precious gift. Let us, rather, heed the words of Jehoshaphat in 2 Chronicles 20:20: "Believe in the Lord your God, and you will be established; believe his prophets, and you will succeed."

---

* All scriptural references in this chapter are from the Revised Standard Version.

---

[1] The expression simply means "Scripture only."
[2] The word means "gifts."
[3] See also 1 Cor. 12:7-11; 14:1-4; Rom. 12:6-8.
[4] Published by the Review and Herald, 1951.
[5] See, for example, *Selected Messages,* book 1, pp. 20, 21.
[6] *The Great Controversy,* pp. xi, xii.
[7] You will find a good summary in *The SDA Bible Commentary,* vol. 3, p. 116.
[8] *The Pulpit Digest,* December 1967.
[9] *King Lear,* Act I, scene 4, line 310.

Born in the tropical West Indies, Roy Adams pastored for many years in Toronto and Montreal. After taking postgraduate studies at Andrews University, he taught theology in the SDA seminary just outside Manila in the Philippines. From there he returned to Canada, where he served for a couple years as associate secretary of the Canadian Union Conference. In 1988 he joined the *Adventist Review* as associate editor. He has two children.

The Great Controversy

*A*ll humanity is now involved in a great controversy between Christ and Satan regarding the character of God, His law, and His sovereignty over the universe. This conflict originated in heaven when a created being, endowed with freedom of choice, in self-exaltation became Satan, God's adversary, and led into rebellion a portion of the angels. He introduced the spirit of rebellion into this world when he led Adam and Eve into sin. This human sin resulted in the distortion of the image of God in humanity, the disordering of the created world, and its eventual devastation at the time of the worldwide flood. Observed by the whole creation, this world became the arena of the universal conflict, out of which the God of love will ultimately be vindicated. To assist His people in this controversy, Christ sends the Holy Spirit and the loyal angels to guide, protect, and sustain them in the way of salvation. (Rev. 12:4-9; Isa. 14:12-14; Eze. 28:12-18; Gen. 3; Rom. 1:19-32; 5:12-21; 8:19-22; Gen. 6-8; 2 Peter 3:6; 1 Cor. 4:9; Heb. 1:14.)—Fundamental Beliefs, No. 8.

CHAPTER SEVEN

By Clifford Goldstein

The Great Controversy
Soldiers in a Great Campaign

We are all soldiers," wrote Justice Oliver Wendell Holmes, "in a great campaign, the details of which are veiled from us. But it is enough for us to know there is a campaign."

The justice had it partly right. We are all indeed "soldiers in a great campaign," but the details have not been veiled. Rather, God has revealed where the campaign began, what issues started it, who the commanders are, our role as "soldiers," how and where the conflict is being fought, and—most important—which side ultimately wins. The campaign even has a name. It is called the great controversy, and though the decisive victory was won 2,000 years ago at Calvary, the battle continues today.

Unfortunately, most people aren't even aware that there's a conflict, much less one that affects their lives and eternal destiny. Millions know about *Star Wars, ET,* the starship *Enterprise,* and Captain Kirk, but few understand anything about the great controversy—a battle that began eons ago in heaven but is being fought here on earth.

"And there was war in heaven: Michael and his angels fought against the dragon; and the dragon fought and his angels, and prevailed not; neither was their place found any more in heaven. And the great dragon was cast out . . . into the earth" (Rev. 12:7-9).

Though Revelation 12, along with Ezekiel 28 and Isaiah 14, vignette Lucifer's fall, Ellen White details it: "Satan was envious and jealous of Jesus Christ. . . . It was the highest crime to rebel against the government of God. All Heaven seemed in commotion.

The angels were marshaled in companies, each division with a higher commanding angel at their head. Satan was warring against the law of God, because [he was] ambitious to exalt himself. . . . The Son of God and true, loyal angels prevailed; and Satan and his sympathizers were expelled from heaven." [1]

As both the Bible and the Spirit of Prophecy attest, the battle didn't end with Satan's eviction from the heavenly courts. On the contrary, the controversy simply moved to the earth, where it has raged furiously ever since. "Woe to the inhabiters of the earth and of the sea! for the devil is come down unto you, having great wrath, because he knoweth that he hath but a short time" (verse 12).

Battle for the Mind

Unlike most wars, however, this battle isn't over land, political ideology, or natural resources; it is, instead, a supernatural struggle between good and evil, right and wrong. "We do not wrestle against flesh and blood, but against principalities, against powers, against the rulers of the darkness of this age, against spiritual hosts of wickedness in the heavenly places" (Eph. 6:12, NKJV). The battle is being waged, not on battlegrounds with missiles, tanks, and helicopters, but in our hearts and minds: "Be sober, be vigilant; because your adversary the devil, as a roaring lion, walketh about, seeking whom he may devour: whom resist stedfast in the faith" (1 Peter 5:8, 9).

The book of Job is a microcosm of this macrocosmic conflict. The story begins with the patriarch enjoying great material prosperity, including a large loving family, reflective of what Eden should have been; above them, however, the struggle between the Lord and Satan raged in heaven, with Satan making accusations against Job. "Doth Job fear God for nought? . . . Put forth thine hand now, and touch all that he hath, and he will curse thee to thy face" (Job 1:9-11).

At first glance Job seems to be the one on trial, but God really is. By impugning Job's motives for being faithful, Satan attacked God Himself. If God was so good, His law so wonderful, would Job serve Him no matter what? Satan implied that Job worshiped God, not because the Lord was worthy, but because it was in Job's best interests to do so. By claiming that Job would turn against Him

60

once things went wrong, Satan, however subtly, insinuated that even Job himself had questions about the character of God. Maybe God wasn't so good after all?

The same basic conflict depicted in Job is fought over every individual. Though expressed under different circumstances, terms, and cultures—and manifested in as many different ways as there are people—we are all, like Job, entangled in this great controversy between Christ and Satan. Though it's a contest for our souls, how often, as with Job, our flesh gets caught in the middle.

Of course, we have not been left to struggle alone. We can no more ourselves defend against the devil than we could with spitballs defend against Stealth bombers. All we can do is daily, consciously place ourselves under the care and protection of Jesus Christ, who not only won the key victory at Calvary but promises to share the fruits of that victory with us. His triumph embraces both earth—"Now thanks be unto God, which always causeth us to triumph in Christ" (2 Cor. 2:14)—and heaven: "And the city had no need of the sun, neither of the moon, to shine in it: for the glory of God did lighten it, and the Lamb is the light thereof. And the nations of them which are saved shall walk in the light of it" (Rev. 21:23, 24).

Calvary—Decisive Battle

Christ's great victory for us was not won when Jesus and His angels ousted Satan and his, nor will it be at the end of the millennium when Satan goes "out to deceive the nations which are in the four quarters of the earth, Gog and Magog, to gather them together to battle: the number of whom is as the sand of the sea" (Rev. 20:8), and is ultimately destroyed. Rather, the victory was won in a Galilean carpenter shop, in a fierce 40-day struggle in the wilderness, in assault after assault among the cities and towns of Judea, in a fearful contest in the Garden of Gethsemane, and finally at the decisive battle at Calvary, when Jesus cried: "It is finished" (John 19:30).

In these engagements Jesus battled, not from the safety, majesty, and comfort of heaven, but in frontline trenches where He faced the full assault of the enemy. Having taken on humanity ("the seed of Abraham" [Heb. 2:16]), Jesus met the devil on the devil's turf: indeed, in heaven Satan caused the fall of a third of the inhabitants; on earth he brought down them all!

Except one. For 33 years Jesus, in human flesh, withstood every barrage of Satan and his legions. Despite endless attempts by Satan to overcome Him, Jesus, at the end of His earthly sojourn, could proclaim: "For the prince of the world cometh, and hath nothing in me" (John 14:30).

The Gospels reveal the intensity of the assaults He faced. In the wilderness Jesus had "fasted forty days and forty nights" (Matt. 4:2). How amazed must Satan have been to see the Lord, with all His power and glory, transformed into a starving, weakened, emaciated human being. God had become part of humanity; Satan had controlled humanity for thousands of years. Jesus, half-dead already, should have been easy prey.

"And when the tempter came to him, he said, If thou be the Son of God, command that these stones be made bread. . . . If thou be the Son of God, cast thyself down. . . . Again, the devil taketh him up into an exceeding high mountain, and sheweth him all the kingdoms of the world, and the glory of them; and saith unto him, All these things will I give unto thee, if thou wilt fall down and worship me" (Matt. 4:3-9).

Here Christ was tempted when He languished in a barren wilderness—a sharp contrast to Adam and Eve, who thrived in a luxurious garden when enticed. Our genetic parents, their bellies filled in a garden shade, succumbed to temptation; our adopted Father, Jesus, His belly hollow in the heat of a desert, didn't.

Yet for Jesus the battle didn't end with the wilderness fast; on the contrary, that experience merely prepared Him for the sorrowful and painful struggle that climaxed at Calvary, where Satan threw his entire force at Jesus because he knew that this was his last chance to win. If he could get Jesus to abandon the plan of salvation, then Christ would have been defeated, the world would have been Satan's, and his accusations against God's government, His mercy, and His justice would have remained forever unanswered. In short, Satan would have won the great controversy!

Meanwhile, as the guilt of every sinner pressed upon His heart, as the malignity of evil separated Him from the Father, as those for whom He was dying taunted "If thou be the Son of God, come down from the cross" (Matt. 27:40)—Jesus knew that if He did come down from the cross, all would be lost. Only by His own death could Christ forever refute Satan's accusations that God could be either merciful or just, but not both. On the cross the Lord proved His justice, because by taking the punishment of sin upon Himself, He would pay the full legal penalty that transgression demanded—and His mercy, because only by paying that penalty Himself could the Lord save sinners from having to pay it themselves.

But with Christ's death, justice and mercy met and triumphed. The destruction of sin and Satan became certain, the redemption of humanity was assured, and the universe was eternally secured. The decisive battle was finished, and there was no question about who ultimately won the great controversy.

War Goes On

Nevertheless, even after Calvary the struggle wasn't over. "Yet Satan was not then destroyed," Ellen White wrote. "The angels did not even then understand all that was involved in the great controversy. The principles at stake were to be more fully revealed." [2]

Even after this display of God's love contrasted to Satan's evil, the Lord wanted to give more understanding to the angels, and He intends to use His people to help provide it: "His intent was that now, *through the church,* the manifold wisdom of God should be made known to the rulers and authorities in the heavenly realms" (Eph. 3:10, NIV).

This verse doesn't diminish Christ's work at the cross, but simply shows that as far as "the rulers and authorities in the heavenly realms" were concerned, all their questions about the "manifold wisdom of God" were not fully answered, even after the death of Jesus, and that the Lord wanted to help answer them "through the church."

Ellen White expresses the same idea: "It becomes every child of God to vindicate His [God's] character." [3] Jesus said it as well: "Herein is my Father glorified, that ye bear much fruit" (John 15:8).

The concept of God being glorified, even vindicated, by His people forms a crucial aspect of present truth. The Seventh-day Adventist Church has been blessed with precious light about Jesus, theology, salvation, education, lifestyle, health, law, grace, and everything pertinent to Christianity—all to prepare a remnant to stand in the great day of God, when the battle between Christ and Satan reaches a crescendo at the end of the ages.

At this time, just before the Second Coming, the Lord will have prepared a people, for "the harvest of the earth is ripe" (Rev. 14:15); in contrast, Satan's "grapes are fully ripe" too (verse 18). Thus, there will be a faithful, obedient people who "keep the commandments of God, and the faith of Jesus" (verse 12), in direct and open contrast to the rest of the world, which is wholly under Satan's power. As the angels view the stunning differences between these two groups, as both righteousness and unrighteousness ripen in the climactic battle of Armageddon, more issues in the great controversy regarding good and evil, Christ and Satan, will be revealed and understood in what Ellen White calls "the final and full display of the love of God." [4]

Each of us, then, has a role in the great controversy, Paul expressed it best when he wrote: "And the God of peace will bruise Satan under your feet shortly" (Rom. 16:20). How is Satan bruised under our soles? Do we literally throw the devil to the ground and kick him? Of course not. Rather, we "bruise Satan" only by a complete surrender to Christ, which allows Him to work in us "both to will and to do of his good pleasure" (Phil. 2:13). A knowledge of the great controversy should bring us to our knees so we, through the power of Christ, can take up "the whole armour of God, that [we] may be able to withstand in the evil day" (Eph. 6:13). Without a daily, conscious walk with Jesus, we can't win the personal battles against sin that can glorify God; indeed, unless we put ourselves on Christ's side, we are on Satan's instead.

As Justice Holmes wrote, we are soldiers in a "great campaign." Our weapons, however, are not guns, tanks, or cruise missiles, but the sword of the Spirit, the breastplate of righteousness, the helmet of salvation, and the shield of faith, all of which come through Jesus, the "captain of [our] salvation" (Heb. 2:10), who has promised to make us "more than conquerors" (Rom. 8:37) through His triumph for us 2,000 years ago on the cross.

---

[1] *The Spirit of Prophecy,* vol. 1, pp. 18-23.
[2] *The Desire of Ages,* p. 761.
[3] *Testimonies,* vol. 5, p. 317.
[4] *The Acts of the Apostles,* p. 9.

Author of seven books, Clifford Goldstein has a M.A. in Hebrew Bible from Johns Hopkins University. He is the editor of *Shabbat Shalom* and the associate editor of *Liberty.* He has a special interest in biblical prophecy. He and his wife live in Columbia, Maryland, with their two young children.

Christ's Ministry in the Heavenly Sanctuary

*T*here is a sanctuary in heaven, the true tabernacle which the Lord set up and not man. In it Christ ministers on our behalf, making available to believers the benefits of His atoning sacrifice offered once for all on the cross. He was inaugurated as our great High Priest and began His intercessory ministry at the time of His ascension. In 1844, at the end of the prophetic period of 2300 days, He entered the second and last phase of His atoning ministry. It is a work of investigative judgment which is part of the ultimate disposition of all sin, typified by the cleansing of the ancient Hebrew sanctuary on the Day of Atonement. In that typical service the sanctuary was cleansed with the blood of animal sacrifices, but the heavenly things are purified with the perfect sacrifice of the blood of Jesus. The investigative judgment reveals to heavenly intelligences who among the dead are asleep in Christ and therefore, in Him, are deemed worthy to have part in the first resurrection. It also makes manifest who among the living are abiding in Christ, keeping the commandments of God and the faith of Jesus, and in Him, therefore, are ready for translation into His everlasting kingdom. This judgment vindicates the justice of God in saving those who believe in Jesus. It declares that those who have remained loyal to God shall receive the kingdom. The completion of this ministry of Christ will mark the close of human probation before the Second Advent. (Heb. 8:1-5; 4:14-16; 9:11-28; 10:19-22; 1:3; 2:16, 17; Dan. 7:9-27; 8:13, 14; 9:24-27; Num. 14:34; Eze. 4:6; Lev. 16; Rev. 14:6, 7; 20:12; 14:12; 22:12.)— Fundamental Beliefs, *No. 23.*

CHAPTER EIGHT
By Richard M. Davidson

A Song for the Sanctuary
Celebrating Its Goodness, Its Truth, Its Beauty

I f you had only one request to make of the Lord, only one goal to seek in life, what would you choose? A whole array of possibilities comes to mind. But in Scripture there is a singular and striking answer to this question. In Psalm 27:4, David unequivocally states: "One thing I ask of the Lord, this is what I seek: that I may dwell in the house of the Lord all the days of my life, to gaze upon the beauty of the Lord and to seek him in his temple (NIV)."

David's singular focus is upon "the house of the Lord"—the sanctuary! When David wrote this psalm, he was "a hunted fugitive, finding refuge in the rocks and caves of the wilderness." [1] His greatest longing was to be continually in the presence of the Lord in His sanctuary. But David's central focus upon the sanctuary was not unique to this time of special circumstances. Many of David's psalms focus upon the sanctuary; in fact, the entire Psalter is really the Hebrew hymnal to be used in worship at the sanctuary.

The whole life of ancient Israel revolved around the sanctuary. At the sanctuary there was joyous commemoration of God's mighty acts of deliverance in the past. From the sanctuary came present forgiveness, peace, assurance. And through the earthly sanctuary the worshiper was pointed upward to the heavenly sanctuary, and forward to the great antitypical Sacrifice and Priest of the heavenly sanctuary.

The Scriptures are replete with sanctuary material. In the Old Testament some 90 chapters are devoted entirely to the subject of the sanctuary, not to mention the 150 psalms comprising the sanctuary hymnody and hundreds of other scattered references to the sanctuary. In the New Testament Gospels and Epistles, the Messiah is repeatedly proclaimed as the one who brings fulfillment to the typical meaning of the sanctuary and its services. His earthly ministry and passion, and His heavenly work, are described largely in the language of the sanctuary. And in the climactic Apocalypse of John, every major section is introduced by a scene from the sanctuary; the entire book is suffused with sanctuary concerns.

Like David and ancient Israel, like the various Bible writers, Adventists since 1844 have had our sights set on the sanctuary. For the Adventist pioneers, "the subject of the sanctuary was the key which unlocked the mystery of the disappointment of 1844. It opened to view a complete system of truth, connected and harmonious, showing that God's hand had directed the great Advent movement and revealing present duty as it brought to light the position and work of His people." [2]

What is the nature of the sanctuary experience that David sought, that ancient Israel embraced, that Adventists treasure? Recently I have been delighted to see how David's singular "psalm for the sanctuary," Psalm 27, in the space of a few verses draws together all the major strands of the sanctuary message and experience. In the process David reveals how the sanctuary message is the encapsulation of the triple star of value in human experience. The philosophers summarize what is of ultimate worth in life in three words: beauty, truth, and goodness. David finds the embodiment of all these in the sanctuary.

Beauty

Psalm 27:4 tells us the first goal of David in the sanctuary experience: "to behold the beauty of the Lord." The Hebrew word *no ῾am,* here translated "beauty," refers to more than abstract aesthetic form. It is a dynamic term, describing beauty that moves the beholder by its loveliness, its pleasantness. Beauty with emotive power—aesthetic experience. David longs to behold this beauty of the Lord in the sanctuary. The psalmist writes elsewhere: "Strength and beauty are in his sanctuary" (Ps. 96:6). "Worship the Lord in the beauty of holiness [or better, in holy beauty]" (Ps. 29:2; 96:9).

A SONG FOR THE SANCTUARY

While a seminary student I first caught a vision of the holy beauty of the Lord in His heavenly sanctuary (especially from Isaiah 6), and as a young pastor, fresh in my "first love" of understanding righteousness by faith, I was introduced to the aesthetic embodiment of the gospel in the types of the Old Testament sanctuary services.[3] The beauty of the gospel in sanctuary typology has continued to shine ever more brilliantly for me in my study, as I have seen how the Old Testament types so forcefully and consistently foreshadow Jesus' substitutionary sacrifice and His high priestly ministry in the heavenly sanctuary.[4] I have been overjoyed to see how every type is fulfilled not only objectively in Jesus, but also how as we are "in Christ," we experientially participate in that fulfillment.

The sanctuary—bastion of beauty!

Truth

Of course, the aesthetic dimension is not the whole. David desires not only "to behold the beauty of the Lord" but also "to enquire in his temple" (Ps. 27:4). The Hebrew word translated "inquire" is *baqar,* a rare word in the Old Testament with a rich meaning. It refers not merely to making inquiry, but has implications of intellectual reflection, of diligent seeking, searching out, detailed examination of evidence to determine the truth of a matter. The sanctuary message is not only an experience of awesome beauty; it is also a reflective, diligent search for truth.

The present truth of the sanctuary message is particularly concentrated in the apocalyptic books of Daniel and Revelation. Books with messages specifically addressed to those living in the last days of earth's history. The sanctuary is at the heart of each of these books.

As the storm of debate over the truthfulness of the sanctuary doctrine has swirled in the Adventist Church throughout the past decade, many have been constrained to reexamine the evidence for the veracity of the sanctuary message proclaimed by the Adventist movement since 1844. The Daniel and Revelation Committee has produced seven volumes during this decade, with much of the material directly relating to the sanctuary. Fresh, exciting insights have emerged from this intense period of intellectual inquiry, which have confirmed the historic Adventist understanding of the biblical material. The basic pillars of this doctrine—the historicist view of prophecy, the year-day principle, the beginning and ending dates for the 2300-day prophecy of Daniel 8:14, the ongoing pre-Advent investigative judgment in the Most Holy Place of the heavenly sanctuary since 1844—all these stand even more firmly in the light of the closest scriptural investigation.[5]

A little more than a decade ago I was ready to leave the Seventh-day Adventist Church because of doubts about the sanctuary doctrine. But over the past few years point by point the objections and questions in my mind have steadily melted away like a hoarfrost before the light of Scripture. My own conviction of the veracity of the historic Adventist position on the sanctuary is stronger than ever before, but now it is a more informed conviction, based upon better biblical evidence than I ever dreamed existed.

The sanctuary—temple of truth!

Goodness

But it is not enough to see the beauty of sanctuary *typology* and the truth of sanctuary eschatology. The sanctuary is not just an object to occupy the mind in aesthetic contemplation or intellectual stimulation. For many Adventists, the sanctuary has been just that—an object to look at, but not a living reality. What is the *relevancy of the sanctuary doctrine?* What difference does it make in our personal lives?

David addresses these questions in verses 5 and 6 of Psalm 27. He introduces the verses with the word "for" or "because" (Heb. *ki*). Here is the practical application of the sanctuary message in his own life: "For in the day of trouble he will keep me safe in his dwelling; he will hide me in the shelter of his tabernacle and set me high upon a rock. Then my head will be exalted above the enemies who surround me." David writes this psalm while he is a fugitive hiding from King Saul. Saul and his army—David's enemies—were malicious witnesses (see verse 12) who had falsely accused David of insurrection against the government. David desperately needed protection in his "day of trouble." He also needed vindication from the false charges brought against him.

For David, the message of the sanctuary was a promise of protection in God's tent, and vindication in His tabernacle.

This is precisely the meaning of the pre-Advent investigative judgment that Adventists have the privilege of proclaiming. In the day of trouble (both present and final) God's people, who trust in His covering, cleansing righteousness, will be protected—"find sanctuary"—in His celestial temple. And from that heavenly sanctuary will come full vindication from false charges against both God's people and their Messiah, the new David, the King of the universe! The meaning of Yom Kippur (Day of Atonement) is indeed good news![6]

David's practical experience of protection and vindication is summarized later in Psalm 27 as "the goodness of the Lord" (verse 13). The thought of God's goodness spontaneously leads David into an experience of joyous worship (verse 6): "At his tabernacle will I sacrifice with shouts of joy; I will sing and make music to the Lord" (NIV).

Adventists have too often become so enamored with the details of the sanctuary typology and symbology, so exercised over the intricacies of eschatological events in the heavenly temple, that they have neglected to praise the goodness of God! But we need only to go to the book of Psalms, where we look into the heart of the true worshiper, and we see that the Holy One is "enthroned on the praises of Israel" (Ps. 22:3, RSV). Both heavenly sanctuary and earthly counterpart are overflowing with paeons of pure praise. The sanctuary is not only soteriology, not only eschatology; it is preeminently and eternally—doxology!

But David's praise was not a frothy emotionalism. He said it was bound up with the bloody sacrifice he offered at the sanctuary (Ps. 27:6). His joy was rooted in the assuring and cleansing blood of the Lamb of God, his substitute and surety. His worship at the sanctuary was a spiral of ever-deepening repentance and ever-heightening joy (Ps. 51). Such worship will be the precious experience of all God's people who are living in "the hour of his judgment" (Rev. 14:7).[7]

The Ultimate Sanctuary Experience

For all that has been said about the importance of the sanctuary, we must hasten to underscore that the apex of the sanctuary message is not the sanctuary itself.

Often in the Psalms (and elsewhere in Scripture) the biblical author structures his literary message in a special pattern called a chiasm. This means that the first half of the psalm is like a mirror image of the second half, with the various parts in reverse parallelism to each other. It also usually means that the central part of the psalm, the climax, indicates the main focus of the psalm. Psalm 27 is composed in this beautiful chiastic structure. What is significant for our purposes here is that the sanctuary, though a prominent feature of this "psalm of the sanctuary," is not the apex. The high point or central focus of the psalm is in verse 8:

You have said, "Seek My face."

My heart says to You, "Your face, Lord, do I seek."

The ultimate meaning of the sanctuary is personal fellowship with the God of the sanctuary. This was made clear when God first gave instructions for building the earthly tabernacle: "And let them make me a sanctuary; that I may dwell among them" (Ex. 25:8). The heavenly sanctuary is where Jesus is now ministering for us; and He *now* invites *us* to enter the sacred celestial precincts by faith, to "seek His face." [8] He invites us spiritually to dwell "in heavenly places" (Eph. 2:6) in the house of the Lord. The sanctuary is not only an object of beauty, a true doctrine, correct behavior, or occasional festival of praise. It is a *way of life,* in constant intimate fellowship with our Beloved in His heavenly abode, His celestial palace.

We can enter now by faith; by faith we can seek His presence, and experience a personal relationship. Yet we wait for the consummation. As did David, we encourage ourselves with the final words of Psalm 27 (verse 14): "Wait for the Lord; be strong, and let your heart take courage; yea, wait for the Lord!" (RSV).

"Wait." The Hebrew word denotes not quiet inactivity, but eager anticipation—standing on tiptoes, as it were, to watch expectantly in hope. If we are in Christ, we do not need to fear the investigative judgment, the time of trouble. Rather, like David (Ps. 26:1; 35:24; 43:1; etc.), we can welcome, even long for, the judgment! With the judgment will come vindication, and the full revelation of the Lord in His sanctuary.

At the end of the antitypical day of atonement, after the

millennium, the camp will be clean. A loud voice from the throne will cry, "Behold, the tabernacle of God is with men!" (Rev. 21:3). The eternal "Feast of Tabernacles" will commence.[9] In fellowship with God, we will gain ever-expanding, incomparable vistas of beauty, truth, and goodness, singing the ultimate "song of the sanctuary."

---

[1] Ellen G. White, *Education,* p. 164.

[2] ———— , *The Great Controversy,* p. 423.

[3] Especially influential were the studies of Leslie Hardinge, now available in his new book, *With Jesus in His Sanctuary* (Harrisburg, Pa: American Cassette Ministries, 1991).

[4] See the author's published dissertation, *Typology in Scripture* (Berrien Springs, Mich.: Andrews University Press, 1981).

[5] See the author's article "In Confirmation of the Sanctuary Message," *Journal of the Adventist Theological Society* 2, No. 1 (Spring 1991): 93-114.

[6] See the author's article "The Good News of Yom Kippur," *Journal of the Adventist Theological Society* 2, No. 2 (Autumn 1991): 4-27.

[7] See my discussion of this "balanced" spiral, and its implications for Adventist lifestyle and worship during the antitypical day of atonement, in "The Good News of Yom Kippur," pp. 13-20.

[8] See the elaboration of this theme especially in Hebrews 4:3, 16; 6:19, 20; 10:19-22; and 12:22-24.

[9] See the author's "Sanctuary Typology," pp. 124-126.

After attending Loma Linda University and the SDA Seminary, Richard M. Davidson began pastoring in the Arizona Conference. Wanting to study the Old Testament more deeply, he returned to Andrews University, where he completed a doctorate in biblical studies. He has been on the seminary faculty since 1979. His most recent book is *A Love Song for the Sabbath.* Whenever he can, he likes to visit the Holy Land to study or to teach in the SDA Jerusalem Center.

The Remnant and Its Mission

*T**he universal church is composed of all who truly believe in Christ, but in the last days, a time of widespread apostasy, a remnant has been called out to keep the commandments of God and the faith of Jesus. This remnant announces the arrival of the judgment hour, proclaims salvation through Christ, and heralds the approach of His second advent. This proclamation is symbolized by the three angels of Revelation 14; it coincides with the work of judgment in heaven and results in a work of repentance and reform on earth. Every believer is called to have a personal part in this worldwide witness. (Rev. 12:17; 14:6-12; 18:1-4; 2 Cor. 5:10; Jude 3, 14; 1 Peter 1:16-19; 2 Peter 3:10-14; Rev. 21:1-14.)—* Fundamental Beliefs, *No. 12.*

CHAPTER NINE
By Hyveth Williams

End-time Living
Our Message, Our Mission

Our generation is perched on the final years of a closing century and the dawn of a new millennium. In spite of all the changes, the promises of economic growth, and the sociological development pronounced by the prophets of a new world order, one cannot help sensing an underlying eeriness suggesting that the caldron of wickedness is boiling over.

These are the best and worst of times, at once both chilling and thrilling. The escalation of deaths in major cities over the past 10 years is a chilling reminder that we are living in the end-time, because those wielding weapons of violence no longer aim to maim but to kill. Consequently, seminars on violence are becoming the vogue in an almost futile gesture to stem the destruction of human life.

These things should not surprise Christians. Our Lord forewarned us to be forearmed with the gospel of truth in a last-day society distinguished by increased lawlessness as people's love grows cold (see Matt. 24:12).

But it is also a thrilling age in which to live. Think of the recent rescue of a renegade satellite by three men positioned in the cargo hold of a spacecraft hundreds of miles above the earth. I remember as a teenager in Jamaica telling my grandmother that one day humans would walk on the moon. At that time she warned me not to speak foolishly or someone might consider me a candidate for an insane asylum.

What an awesome age in which to live! How can we make Adventism relevant to the generation living in the end-time?

75

Some Adventists think we should prepare people to survive last-day events by planning escapades into the forests and mountains. But look at the megatechnological advances of the past few decades. Humanity now has instruments that register the heat left by people up to 24 hours after they've left a location, chemicals that can defoliate whole forests, lasers able to penetrate and explode large rocks, and amphibious vehicles and marine mammals trained to detect and destroy targets. Computers talk to us and communicate with each other in sophisticated scientific languages. Satellites stalk the heavens, delivering instant portraits pinpointing events on any part of our planet, such as the stunning photos of the movement of Iraqi troops during Operation Desert Storm. Obviously we must create alternatives to comfort one another without the traditional safety of the "hills and forests." How then shall we live in the end-time?

Not long ago I shared a long flight with a prominent physician. He ordered a drink and offered to buy me one. When I declined, he confessed that he needed the alcohol to numb his fear of being held hostage in flight. I explained that I was a minister, at which time he described himself as a once-devout Catholic who was so disillusioned with his religion that he was currently searching for a church to renew his faith. Imagine the intensity of my heartbeat as he told stories of congregations to which his search had led him.

I was eager to introduce him to Adventism, but when I did I was stunned by his gracious rejection, laced with compliments for our advances in the medical field. He had many friends and colleagues who had been born and raised Adventist but, like himself, had distanced themselves from their religious roots because these seemed no more relevant to their needs than the Catholic Church to his. He poignantly confessed his spiritual poverty and asked what the contemporary clergy intend to do to make religion relevant to him and his colleagues living with the vivid evidence of moral, spiritual, mental, and physical decline—indisputable signs that humanity is rapidly running out of time. As pastor of a congregation composed of 56 percent young professionals returning to the church after decades of absence, I've responded to this question repeatedly.

Adventism *is* relevant and appealing! We need not compromise issues of faith to attract and maintain members. The very message of the Second Coming that energized our founders and caused the Seventh-day Adventist Church to rise out of the religious complacency and disillusionment in the middle nineteenth century is still empowering. However, we must keep this message contemporary, convicting, and convincing by renewing our commitment to several biblical perspectives.

1. Worship

God gives the church militant the Word of God amid the battle cry "The hour of his judgment has come" (Rev. 14:7, NIV). He calls mankind to come out of religious confusion and to "worship him who made the heavens, the earth, the sea and the springs of water" (verse 7, NIV).

The word "worship" literally means to regard someone with an expression of deep love, motivated, in God's case, by awe, reverence, and respect. It also means to prostrate oneself before a royal person, to pay homage or make obeisance. Worship, in content and practice, must combine all these to be one of the pillars of faith for the last-day church that will be triumphant in the end.

Without restating the arguments for or against a traditional worship style, we must agree that the time has come for a healthy change in congregational worship in the Adventist Church. We need to move from our primarily Eurocentric, human-centered style in which songs and sermons focus on "I" to a God-centered style that is inclusive or at least reflective of the many cultures, customs, and peoples who embrace Adventism. While the foundation, center, and circumference of our worship is the Holy Trinity, whenever people attend our worship they should be able to detect our fundamental beliefs. For instance, baptism should not be something added to a service, but the whole event should reflect what we believe about baptism. To accomplish this, I recommend that every church establish a worship committee that reflects the congregation theologically, socially, and gender- and agewise to plan spiritually impressive worship events that highlight the wonder, witness, and warfare of the last-day church.

We must accept the charge of Revelation 14:7 to be inclusive of worship. The Bible challenges us to be innovative and Christ-centered so that others in the Christian community may appeal to our church for guidance in truly theocentric worship, instead of our seeking their options.

2. Human Sexuality

Seventh-day Adventists living in the end-time must develop a biblically based doctrine of human sexuality as it relates to the plan of salvation. Both our clergy and congregations are suffering from the damaging effects of irresponsible or uninformed sexual choices. Over the past five years I've conducted Weeks of Prayer in the United States, the West Indies, New Zealand, and Australia. Each time, I've asked participants to write questions that are of utmost concern, regardless of the topic, and submit these anonymously for possible inclusion in a session. To date, I've collected more than 500 questions to use in an upcoming book. Seventy percent of the questions are about sexuality, 20 percent about religion, and 10 percent about various lifestyle issues, such as jewelry, movies, and makeup.

My seminar "Human Sexuality in the Plan of Salvation," a discussion about contemporary sexual practices and biblical injunctions, exposes problems of premarital sex, abortion, sexual abuse, and homosexuality. Young people carry tremendous guilt, and for many the answer is to end association with a church that does not appear to relate to their trauma but compounds it with perceived rigorous religious demands.

The majority of our young people attempt to be whole in a broken society. But we can no longer avoid confronting this challenge with compassionate biblical answers to counteract secular suggestions about human sexuality.

More and more adult Adventists are consciously choosing to embrace a homosexual lifestyle. Some ministers use their clerical office to disguise sexual promiscuity, which is creating an unspoken amount of tension in congregations. Increasingly, members who have experienced varying degrees of sexual contact with ministers, some suffering irreparable psychological trauma, are seeking counsel, but we need resources to prevent rather than cure after the fact. Likewise, sexual abuse of children is an iceberg waiting to emerge in fundamental Christian communities.

78

These incidents make quite clear that the church has no other choice than to develop a teaching instrument on sexuality that can be used in our schools and churches to properly educate and remind our people of God's way in an age obsessed with lust and irresponsible sexuality.

3. Social Action

I was thrilled with the swift, courageous, compassionate action of the North American Division in response to the riots in Los Angeles. However, it's unfortunate that it had to take such a devastating event to make us become socially relevant. While I commend ADRA and other ministries for their work in foreign lands, I believe that we have no other choice but to make feeding the hungry and sheltering the homeless a priority so that our preaching and praying may evolve into practical social actions that would at least ease some of the anguish and tensions of this evil age.

I have a burden for victims of AIDS—I'm afraid we haven't done enough in this area. When I visit patients with AIDS, I'm constantly amazed at how many, including Adventists (past and present), are cut off from family and friends and left to die alone. While I believe that we should preach without apology the biblical denunciation of homosexual practice as well as heterosexual promiscuity, we cannot allow homophobia to separate us from our families, whether spiritual or biological, at such a critical time.

Remember, Jesus warned that these are only the beginning of the pangs. If we are alert, we must admit that something even more wicked lurks on the horizon for people living in the end-time. If the medical prognosticators are correct, the year 2000 will be hell on earth as the AIDS epidemic claims millions of victims (up to 120 million, according to world health organizations) who are even now unaware that they are carriers of the deadly disease. Many of these are converted men and women who, though they have forsaken a life of sin, bear in their bodies its results. We cannot forsake them when they fall victim to this silent killer, especially if we accept the assurance in John 3:16 that Jesus has guaranteed that no true believer will perish (the second death) but have everlasting life.

We don't have to wait for an edict or an emergency encyclical from our church headquarters to exercise our divine mandate (Matt. 25:34-40) for social action. Every local congregation can do its part in its sphere of influence. For example, at the Boston Temple we open our facilities every day to the community. Not long ago a neighbor seeking a place to pray about his out-of-control life was led to accept Jesus Christ as his personal Saviour and now attends church regularly. We've also started a project to feed and clothe the hungry and homeless, and so far two persons we've assisted attend Sabbath services. We rent our fellowship halls to community groups and different city council agencies, and a few months ago a local condominium consortium requested that we present a stop-smoking seminar to their clients. They are coming to us to seek our expertise in these areas, and we no longer have any other choice than to become socially active in our various communities.

4. Preaching

In the nineteenth century Ellen White reported: "Today there is need of the voice of stern rebuke; for grievous sins have separated the people from God. Infidelity is fast becoming fashionable. . . . The smooth sermons so often preached make no lasting impression; the trumpet does not give a certain sound. Men are not cut to the heart by the plain, sharp truth of God's Word." [1] Charles Swindoll describes the perpetual pulpit trauma in the contemporary church as the fine art of talking in someone else's sleep. We all dreamed that this age would be the zenith of preaching because of the many dramatic demonstrations that we are living in the end-time. But for many congregations it's still a dream.

Ellen White suggests that "the object of preaching is not alone to convey information, not merely to convince the intellect. The preaching of the Word should appeal to the intellect, and should impart knowledge, but it should do more than this. The words of the minister should reach the hearts of the hearers." [2] We Adventists have no other choice than to make preaching incarnational for this generation living in the end-time. In 20 to 40 minutes the preacher must make the Word of God take on flesh and dwell among us.

80

END-TIME LIVING

Adventists have a message, and we should preach it without reservation or apology. People need to hear the undiluted strains of the blessed hope ringing from the pulpits of the Adventist Church, calling the soldiers enlisted in the army of Christ to militant action, as we are engaged in the final conflict of the "great controversy."

Because our generation has the advantage of the accumulated records of all preceding ages of sacred and secular history, plus the blessing and burden of living in the end-time when all the purposes of God will be climaxed by the second coming of Christ, we have no other choice: we must restate and clarify our mission so that people may be called to Christianity in the Seventh-day Adventist experience. We cannot fail our God now!

---

[1] *Prophets and Kings,* p. 140.
[2] *Testimonies to Ministers,* p. 62.

 Senior pastor of the Boston Temple, Hyveth Williams was born in Jamaica, raised in London, and is now a citizen of the United States. She was a radio talk show host, television producer, and executive assistant to the mayor of Hartford, Connecticut. After a dramatic conversion in 1977, she was baptized into the Seventh-day Adventist Church and earned theological degrees at Columbia Union College and the SDA Seminary. Pastor Williams was named an Outstanding Young Woman of America, and was honored by the Connecticut General Assembly for her community services.

Spiritual Gifts and Ministries

God bestows upon all members of His church in every age spiritual gifts which each member is to employ in loving ministry for the common good of the church and of humanity. Given by the agency of the Holy Spirit, who apportions to each member as He wills, the gifts provide all abilities and ministries needed by the church to fulfill its divinely ordained functions. According to the Scriptures, these gifts include such ministries as faith, healing, prophecy, proclamation, teaching, administration, reconciliation, compassion, and self-sacrificing service and charity for the help and encouragement of people. Some members are called of God and endowed by the Spirit for functions recognized by the church in pastoral, evangelistic, apostolic, and teaching ministries particularly needed to equip the members for service, to build up the church to spiritual maturity, and to foster unity of the faith and knowledge of God. When members employ these spiritual gifts as faithful stewards of God's varied grace, the church is protected from the destructive influence of false doctrine, grows with a growth that is from God, and is built up in faith and love. (Rom. 12:4-8; 1 Cor. 12:9-11, 27, 28; Eph. 4:8, 11-16; Acts 6:1-7; 1 Tim. 2:1-3; 1 Peter 4:10, 11.)—Fundamental Beliefs, No. 16.

The Ministry of the Laity
"Minister" Is a Verb, Not a Noun.

I grew up in the home of typical Seventh-day Adventist laypeople, or so I thought. As long as I can remember, my father always served our local church in such capacities as Sabbath school teacher, elder, personal ministries leader, treasurer, and Pathfinder Club staff member. And my mother was at times a deaconess, children's Sabbath school leader, and Dorcas Society leader. I thought all church families were like ours.

Only after I served as a church pastor for some time did I discover that many church members prefer the role of religious consumers and do not see themselves as ministers. I am always unnerved by those who refer to my clergy status as "minister" rather than "pastor." We are all ministers. "Minister" is a verb, not a noun.

Seventh-day Adventists believe that the mission of Christ is equally the responsibility of every person who trusts in Him. "To each one . . . is given" some ability to serve in Christ's name (1 Cor. 12:7).* And everyone has some role in the ministry of Christ's good news.

Unlike other religions of the time of the New Testament, the Christian faith was not conceived as an organization in which professional priests served a clientele. "But you are . . . a royal priesthood . . . that you may declare the praises of him who called you out of darkness into his wonderful light" (1 Peter 2:9). The early church did not have designated ministers who conducted sacrifices for the profane and less holy. Instead, all the followers of

83

Christ were urged "to offer their bodies as living sacrifices, holy and pleasing to God—this is your spiritual act of worship" (Rom. 12:1).

Seventh-day Adventists expect every church member to participate in the work of ministry. "A working church is a growing church," observes Ellen White. She says that it is the purpose of the pastor "to get the full membership of the church actively engaged in the various departments of church work" (*Gospel Workers,* p. 198). Pastors "can never perform the work that the church should do" (*Testimonies,* vol. 4, p. 69).

Those members who are not called to be pastors have a unique ministry—to convey God's compassion and truth beyond the community of faith into the secular world.

I learned this the hard way during a time that I worked for a public service agency. During the first several weeks some of my largely unchurched coworkers easily shared concerns, needs in their lives, and even profound spiritual questions. They eagerly listened to Adventist ideas and Bible texts that I shared with them. Then I mentioned to one trusted colleague that I was on a leave of absence from the pastorate. Quickly the word spread, and conversations became guarded; coworkers were friendly but closed. My opportunities for ministry evaporated.

The false concepts of "clergy" and "laity" have permeated our culture. Only a minister who is not clergy, who is not "a religious person," can break through that attitudinal barrier. That is the ministry to which the Holy Spirit calls every believer.

"I will send you a Comforter," Christ promised as He prepared to leave His followers in this world (see John 15:26). This Comforter, "the Holy Spirit, whom the Father will send in my name, will teach you all things" (John 14:26). Specifically, the Holy Spirit provides "gifts" that enable believers to engage in service (see 1 Cor. 12:4, 5).

Every believer receives gifts that are "to prepare God's people for works of service, so that the body of Christ may be built up" (Eph. 4:12). The New Testament provides many examples of spiritual gifts—teaching, evangelism, compassion, encouragement, philanthropy, management, healing, leadership, hospitality, and even the diligent care for details; but there is no indication that the list is any way limited.

By living into the gifts that the Holy Spirit supplies, the individual believer experiences the work of the Spirit in his or her life. The gifts "prepare God's people for works of service . . . *until we all reach unity in the faith and in the knowledge of the Son of God and *become mature,* attaining to the whole measure of the fullness of Christ" (verses 12, 13). As the believer allows the Spirit to lead in a life of service, entering fully into Christ's ministry, he or she evidences "the fruit of the Spirit"—a character that includes "love, joy, peace, patience, kindness, goodness, faithfulness, gentleness and self-control" (Gal. 5:22, 23).

"Let ministers teach church members that in order to grow in spirituality, they must carry the burden that the Lord has laid upon them," urged Ellen White (*Gospel Workers,* p. 200). "God bestows various talents and gifts upon men, not that they may lie useless, nor that they may be employed in amusements or selfish gratification, but that they may be a blessing to others by enabling men to do earnest, self-sacrificing missionary work," she commented in an article in the *Youth's Instructor,* November 6, 1902.

Some of the most gifted ministers I have ever met, men and women who humble me, are volunteers, church members who labor quietly day in and day out, not seeking institutional support or making theological pronouncements. God works through them in powerful ways!

Gus Newman worked as a carpenter at Gulf Oil Corporation. He had a secure, well-paying job in the depths of the Depression. However, he resigned to give himself to feeding the hungry and reaching the hopeless in the inner city. I had the privilege of working with him when he was in his late 80s at the old Boston Mission.

Every day he put in long hours gathering dented cans and scarred produce from wholesale grocers, repairing and recycling cast-off furniture, and making the rounds of his flock of street drunks, aged poor, retarded children, undocumented immigrants, and disabled folk—ignored and locked out by a bustling metropolis. He had a patient ear, a loving hand on the shoulder, and a word of encouragement for everyone. He also could be the "Dutch uncle" when necessary.

The courage of Brother Newman in that dangerous neighborhood was legendary. He would pursue a fleeing shoplifter right into a bar and confront her regarding the stolen items on her person. Once he simply grabbed the blade of a knife with which a young robber, high on drugs, was threatening him. "I would rather cut my hand than get a chest wound," he told me later.

Every Sabbath afternoon he led a branch Sabbath school in the mission. Over the years, scores accepted Christ into their lives and were baptized into the church. Gus Newman was a living monument of hope walking pitiless and uncaring streets. He gave his life, in Christ's name, to those most of us would consider beneath concern.

The gospel demands our life. That is more difficult than assenting to 27 doctrines or carefully observing 14 church standards. Christ confronts our nice churches and comfortable, respectable lives. "I want all of you," He says. "I want your passion and creativity, your skills and influence, your integrity and character. I need you in your wholeness, imperfect though you are, to illustrate to those whom I love who I really am."

For an Adventist, no career is ever really a vocation. Adventist physicians are not just physicians, but something more. They don't wear pith helmets and live in thatched huts—theirs is the world of corporate medicine and laser surgery—but they are still "missionary doctors." Or "missionary day-care workers," or "missionary data processing directors," or . . . The blessed hope pervades all that we do.

When we offer ourselves as "living sacrifices" to Christ, He changes all that we do and all that we are. I learned that this is a powerful, even dangerous, business!

I baptized Katherine Iannelli about 11 years ago, while I was pastor of the Allentown, Pennsylvania, Seventh-day Adventist Church. I met her first in a stress seminar. She had heard about the Adventist Church through a health outreach, and later she joined a small group Bible study. Several of our lay Bible ministers visited her and she asked for baptism during a Bible seminar.

Kathy and I talked about what it meant for her to give her

whole life to Christ, and she took it very seriously. Just how seriously I didn't learn until last year.

"As a journalist, I've dealt with enough senseless slayings to numb the nerves and dull the eye," wrote Rich Brust in the January 17, 1991, Allentown *Morning Call.* "But there's something about the painful case of Kathy Iannelli that I continue to turn over in my thoughts."

"I never knew anyone like Kathy," Brust quotes her friends. "She took the gospel to heart; some people read it, but she practiced it. . . . Iannelli took in strays—relatives with marital problems, friends who were backward and shy. . . . Any holiday she would gather homeless people at her house."

One of her missionary projects the column described was Edwin Soto, a friend who had struggled for a long time with depression and drugs. "The odds were against her. Last week her body was found in her Allentown apartment." Soto had killed her and then committed suicide.

"But to grasp the full tragedy of Iannelli's death, you need to know how she lived," writes the journalist. "To the devout, religious Iannelli, Soto was just another human being who needed her." She met him through a family in the church. She helped him quit drugs, but he often relapsed, stealing from her. Her friends urged her to throw him out. She thought she saw a glimmer of hope, so she would ask, "Would Jesus throw him out?"

Kathy lived from a powerful hope—the Advent hope—which gave her a new vision of the people around her and how life could be. And it caught the eye of a hardened, secular journalist.

If we are honest with ourselves, it is more difficult to give our lives day by day to Christ than it is to give up life all at once. In fact, those of us who live the most orderly and safe lives sometimes have the hardest times finding Christ at work in our lives.

He is there, asking to be involved in our jobs, our relationships, our recreation, our plans, and our possessions. He gently invites us each day to lift up our eyes and catch the vision He has of a life in which we struggle against narrowness, routine, numbness, and materialism. He calls us to a life of joy, compassion, justice, and creativity.

"I have purchased your life with My own blood," Jesus tells me.

"I have given it back to you so that you might use it in a truly powerful way. I have knelt to wash your feet. Kneel with Me to wash the feet of others for whom I have given My life."

The life of service is a core value of the Adventist faith. I grew up to fervent prayers that I would go as a missionary. I have discovered that we live in a global village and that there are just as many "heathen" around the block as there are around the globe. I do not want my children to grow up thinking that you have to get a paycheck from a denominational organization to be a minister. My parents did not believe that, but I sometimes fear that my generation does.

God calls each of us. Our work has eternal value because God chooses to accomplish His purposes through our words and deeds. God cares about the quality of life, and He has a plan for your life. God cares about the person sitting in the car next to you at the stoplight, and He has a plan for that life, too. He may have in mind that the two lives will touch in a way that allows His life-changing power to spark through you to the other.

Minister is a verb, not a noun.

---

* Texts in this chapter are from the New International Version.

An ordained minister, Monte Sahlin is adult ministries coordinator in the Church Ministries Department of the North American Division. He oversees the development and resourcing of programs in church growth, lay witnessing, community service, adult Sabbath school, family life, and such specialized areas of ministry as prison ministries and disaster services. He and his wife have two daughters.

The Remnant and Its Mission

*T*he universal church is composed of all who truly believe in Christ, but in the last days, a time of widespread apostasy, a remnant has been called out to keep the commandments of God and the faith of Jesus. This remnant announces the arrival of the judgment hour, proclaims salvation through Jesus Christ, and heralds the approach of His second advent. This proclamation is symbolized by the three angels of Revelation 14; it coincides with the work of judgment in heaven and results in a work of repentance and reform on earth. Every believer is called to have a personal part in this worldwide witness. (Rev. 12:17; 14:6-12; 18:1-4; 2 Cor. 5:10; Jude 3, 14; 1 Peter 1:16-19; 2 Peter 3:10-14; Rev. 21:1-14.)—Fundamental Beliefs, *No. 12.*

CHAPTER ELEVEN

By William H. Shea and
Clifford Goldstein

1844
A People of Prophecy

Even with the choicest timber, finest brick, and best workers, if the foundation isn't steady, the house will fall. And even if the foundation's firm, if it doesn't sit on solid ground, the structure will crumble anyway.

The same with the house that Adventism has built. If the sanctuary message with its 1844 dating, the foundation of the house, is not solid, the house isn't either. Fortunately, not only is that foundation set in cement; it sits on the Rock, Jesus Christ.

Resting on Jesus

The 1844 date for the beginning of the pre-Advent judgment rests squarely on Jesus Christ. The ninth chapter of the book of Daniel centers on the 70-week prophecy, which is by far the most important and convincing Messianic prediction in the Bible. Yet this crucial 70-week prophecy is only part of the larger 2300-day prophecy of the investigative judgment. If the 1844 investigative judgment were not crucial, why would the Lord have so inextricably linked it to such an important prophecy as the 70 weeks? The answer, of course, is that He wouldn't have.

Are Seventh-day Adventists hung up on dates? No. However, the Bible clearly ties Christ's work for us with specific dates. More than 500 years before Christ, Daniel 9:24-27 gave the exact years when Jesus would begin His ministry and when He would be crucified. That prediction is like someone in 1492 (the year Columbus took off for India and found America instead) predicting

91

that George Bush would be elected president of the United States in 1988.

The prophecy begins with a time period, 70 weeks that were "cut off" upon Daniel's people and their holy city, Jerusalem (verse 24).[1] The second verse of this prophecy (verse 25) gives the starting point of those 70 weeks: "From the going forth of the command to restore and build Jerusalem until Messiah the Prince, there shall be seven weeks and sixty-two weeks [or 69 weeks]" (NKJV).

When did this word go forth "to restore and build Jerusalem"? There are only four possibilities:

Text	King	Date	Subject
Ezra 1	Cyrus	538 B.C.	Return of the people; rebuilding the Temple
Ezra 6	Darius	520 B.C.	Reaffirms Cyrus' decree to rebuild the Temple
Ezra 7	Artaxerxes I	457 B.C.	Return with Ezra; authority to Ezra
Nehemiah 2	Artaxerxes I	444 B.C.	Authority to Nehemiah as governor of Judea

The first two of these decrees resulted only in the reconstruction of the Temple, which was completed in 516/515 B.C. (Ezra 6:15-18). They, therefore, don't meet the requirements of the prophecy.

In the third choice, found in Ezra 7, Ezra was given permission to reconstruct the city. How do we know? Because people living in the area of Jerusalem wrote to Artaxerxes, saying: "The Jews who came up to us *from you* have gone to Jerusalem and are *rebuilding that rebellious and wicked city*. They are restoring the walls and repairing the foundations" (Ezra 4:12, NIV).

Obviously, the Jews who came up "from you," meaning Artaxerxes, were rebuilding "that rebellious and wicked city." The only decree the Bible mentions as coming from Artaxerxes that fits is the one in Ezra 7 (the chapters in Ezra are not in chronological order), which was given in Artaxerxes' seventh year. (The decree for Nehemiah dealt only with continuing what Ezra had already started, and thus is ruled out as well.)

From a variety of ancient sources, including an eclipse text, we know that Artaxerxes' father, Xerxes, was murdered in 465 B.C. The new king's first full and official year did not begin until the next new year, in the spring of 464 B.C., which means—in terms of the Jewish calendar used then—that the seventh year of Artaxerxes extended from the fall (about September-October) of 458 B.C. to the fall of 457 B.C. Thus, the starting date of the 70 weeks is 457 B.C.

Therefore, from the command "to restore and build Jerusalem [457 B.C.] until Messiah the Prince [Jesus]" would be 69 weeks. Because a *literal* 69 weeks is only about a year and four months, the prophecy would have the Messiah coming in 455 B.C. if literal time were used. Obviously, the day-year principle must be applied.[2] Because 69 weeks equals 483 days (69 × 7), a day for a year comes to 483 years. Thus, the command "to restore and build Jerusalem until Messiah the Prince" would be 483 years, which comes to A.D. 27 (remember to delete the zero year on the calendar). Amazingly enough, this is the time that Jesus did begin His earthly ministry.

The final "week," or seven years, of the prophecy, dealt with the death of Jesus ("in the midst of the week," three and a half years later, He would be cut off) and the covenant relationship between Israel and the Lord. The seventy weeks, then, end in A.D. 34 (see chart).

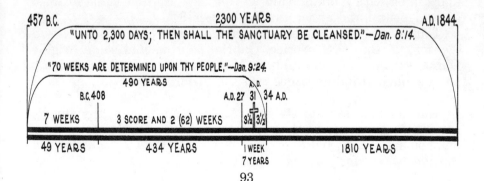

The 2300 Days

So the 70-week prophecy, which gives us a definite starting date, is based literally on Jesus. He is the surety that the prophecy is true. Scripture, however, says that the 70 weeks—457 B.C. to A.D. 34—are "cut off." Cut off from what?

The answer is found in the preceding chapter. Here we should note carefully the two words for "vision"—one indicating the whole vision, the other a part of it. "In the third year of the reign of king Belshazzar a vision [chazon] appeared unto me" (Dan. 8:1). In that vision Daniel sees a ram, then a goat, then a terrible little horn power, and finally the vision ends with the proclamation, "Unto two thousand and three hundred days [evenings/mornings]; then shall the sanctuary be cleansed" (verse 14).

Daniel is then given an explanation of the vision. The ram is Media-Persia (verse 20), the goat Greece (verse 21), and the little horn a terrible persecuting power (verses 23-25), obviously the Roman Empire. Daniel is not given, however, any information about the 2300 evenings and mornings part of the prophecy. Gabriel, the angel who was interpreting for Daniel, said: "The vision [mareh] of the evening and the morning which was told is true" (verse 26). Daniel, however, wrote: "I was astonished at the vision [mareh], but none understood it" (verse 27). Because everything else in Daniel 8 was explained, the only thing he didn't understand was the vision (mareh) of the 2300 days.

In chapter 9 Gabriel reappears: "Yea, whiles I was speaking in prayer, even the man Gabriel, whom I had seen in the vision [chazon] at the beginning . . . touched me. And he informed me, and talked with me, and said, O Daniel, I am now come forth to give thee skill and understanding" (Dan. 9:21, 22).

Daniel here refers to the same angel he had seen in the vision (chazon) of Daniel 8. Notice, Gabriel said he had come to give Daniel skill and understanding. The last time Daniel needed any special understanding concerned the vision (mareh) of the 2300 days.

Gabriel then says to Daniel: "At the beginning of thy supplications the commandment came forth, and I am come to shew thee, for thou are greatly beloved: therefore understand the matter, and consider the vision [mareh]" (verse 23).

What *mareh?* The *mareh* of the 2300 days that Daniel hadn't understood from the previous chapter. Thus, we have the same angel interpreter as in Daniel 8. Gabriel then promises to give Daniel understanding, and the last thing recorded in the Bible that he didn't understand was the *mareh* of the 2300 evenings and mornings. Gabriel points him specifically to that *mareh* and tells him to "understand" it, then he gives him the 70-week prophecy. Clearly, the vision in Daniel 9 is linked to the one in Daniel 8.

Also, what type of prophecy was the *mareh* in Daniel 8? A time prophecy. In Daniel 9, after Gabriel points Daniel to the *mareh,* what does he give him? Another time prophecy: "Seventy weeks," Gabriel says, "are [cut off] upon thy people and upon thy holy city" (verse 24). Obviously, they are "cut off" from the larger 2300-evening/morning prophecy of Daniel 8.

1844 Established

With 457 B.C.—the starting point of the 70 weeks, which are "cut off" from the 2300 days—the end of the 2300-evening/morning prophecy (again using the day-year principle) comes to the year 1844. Simply add 2300 years to 457 B.C. (remember to delete the zero year on the calendar), and you get the date. Or you can start with the end of the 70 weeks (490 years), which is A.D. 34, and add the remaining 1810 years of the 2300. That too comes to 1844.[3] (See chart.)

Two points need to be reiterated. First, the 2300-day prophecy is based on Jesus Himself. Second, because this prophecy is so inextricably linked to the 70 weeks, the 2300-day prophecy must be crucial as well.

It is. The 70-week prophecy depicts a crucial stage in the plan of salvation: the death of Jesus as the sacrifice for the sins of the world. The 2300 days depicts another crucial stage in the plan of salvation: the judgment in heaven preceding the Second Coming. Both events, the sacrifice and the judgment, are part of the same prophecy because both portray either the work of Jesus for us, first as the "lamb of God" (John 1:29); or second, His work as the high priest in the heavenly sanctuary (Heb. 9:11, 12).

The two prophecies are inextricably linked for another reason: the work that Jesus did for us on the cross is what gets us through the judgment. Christ stands as our advocate (1 John 2:1), pleading His righteousness in the "presence of God *for us*" (Heb. 9:24). Yet He can be our advocate, our substitute, our surety, during the judgment of the 2300 days only because of what He accomplished for us during those 70 weeks.[4]

Thus, the relevancy of the 2300 days cannot be separated from the relevancy of the 70 weeks. The work that Christ did on the cross, the work that He is doing in the judgment, will affect every one of us. Either we have surrendered ourselves to Jesus, *by faith,* to be justified by His blood, pardoned, and ultimately cleansed from our sins, or we will stand without a substitute on the day of judgment. Either we have been born again and, *by faith,* renewed by the power of Christ to change our lives, or we will have spurned His sanctifying power to "cleanse us from all unrighteousness" (1 John 1:9). Either we have placed ourselves *by faith* under the garments of His righteousness or we will stand without a covering, in the shame of our own nakedness.

Ultimately, the 2300-day prophecy is crucial because it reveals whether we have truly accepted, *by faith,* what Christ accomplished for us during the 70 weeks.

If we are Christians, we "may have boldness in the day of judgment" (1 John 4:17). We can have confidence that Jesus is our surety, judge, and advocate. And as the Bible clearly teaches, we can have the confidence that Jesus is the Rock upon which not only our salvation but our church rests as well.

---

[1] For a deeper study on why the translation "cut off" is correct, see "The Relationship Between the Prophecies of Daniel 8 and 9," *The Sanctuary and the Atonement* (Review and Herald, 1981).

[2] For a fuller study of the day-year principle, see William Shea, *Selected Studies on Prophetic Interpretation* (General Conference of SDA, 1982).

[3] See also Clifford Goldstein, *1844 Made Simple* (Pacific Press, 1988).

[4] ———, *False Balances* (Pacific Press, 1992).

Author of seven books, Clifford Goldstein has a M.A. in Hebrew Bible from Johns Hopkins University. He is the editor of *Shabbat Shalom* and the associate editor of *Liberty*. He has a special interest in biblical prophecy. He and his wife live in Columbia, Maryland, with their two young children.

William H. Shea began his career as a medical doctor, serving in the Inter-American Division for eight years. Then, studying archaeology and ancient history, he obtained a Ph.D. from the University of Michigan in 1976. He speaks English and Spanish and reads German and French, as well as Hebrew and other Semitic languages. He is currently a research associate at the Biblical Research Institute in the General Conference.

Stewardship

We are God's stewards, entrusted by Him with time and opportunities, abilities and possessions, and the blessings of the earth and its resources. We are responsible to Him for their proper use. We acknowledge God's ownership by faithful service to Him and our fellow men, and by returning tithes and giving offerings for the proclamation of His gospel and the support and growth of His church. Stewardship is a privilege given to us by God for nurture in love and the victory over selfishness and covetousness. The steward rejoices in the blessings that come to others as a result of his faithfulness. (Gen. 1:26-28; 2:15; 1 Chron. 29:14; Haggai 1:3-11; Mal. 3:8-12; 1 Cor. 9:9-14; Matt. 23:23; Rom. 15:26, 27.)— Fundamental Beliefs, No. 20.

CHAPTER TWELVE

By Myron Widmer

Partners With God
We Manage, but God Owns

Mention stewardship, and many Christians cringe. They are afraid that someone is going to ask them to give more money.

In reality it is not someone but Someone who is doing the asking, and money is the least of what He wants. He asks for *everything* a person has and is. He wants it all dedicated to His cause on earth.

But somewhere along the line the word "stewardship" got all tangled up with simply money. You've heard the comments, and so have I. Whenever the church budget runs low, someone usually pipes up, "Let's have a stewardship campaign. That'll raise the funds!"

Well, it might raise the funds, but such brash reasoning limits the biblical concept of what stewardship is all about. For stewardship isn't about money. It's about a *relationship,* a trust relationship between the Creator and His creation.

To believe in stewardship is to affirm that God exists. And to affirm God's existence is to believe in stewardship. They are inextricably tied together, for at the basis of all stewardship is the fact that God exists and that He is Creator (Gen. 1:1), Owner (Ps. 24:1), Sustainer (Heb. 1:3; Acts 17:28), and Redeemer (Ps. 19:14) of us and the entire universe.

With this understanding, Adventist Christians see humans as simply stewards, or *managers* for God of all that He entrusts to us while we exist on earth. That includes our time, talents, physical and mental health, material possessions, and environment.

99

As one would guess, stewardship isn't a real popular message with today's crowd. Culture has done well in conditioning even Christians to equate success with the acquisition of money, material possessions, power, and prestige—unapologetic self-centeredness at its best!

The natural consequence is Christians who begin to paint pictures of God with brushes tainted by selfish agendas. They sometimes view God as "a television game show host" who dispenses and withholds life's prizes.[1] Or as "a gigantic cosmic bellhop whose sole duty it is to indulge our desires, spare us inconveniences, and ensure our success in every venture."[2]

Nothing, however, could be more antithetical, more diametrically opposed to the biblical portrayal of God and of the radically different life He calls His followers to pursue. The world even laughs at the seemingly outrageous call of God for Christians to live a life of giving.

But what is a paradox to the world God says makes good sense. He says that when we lose our life in service to God, we will truly find it (Luke 9:24). Paul even asks us to become a sacrifice for God, a *living* sacrifice. "I appeal to you . . . to present your bodies as a living sacrifice, holy and acceptable to God, which is your spiritual worship" (Rom. 12:1).*

Wow! Does that mean that God doesn't want us to have any fun, any happiness, or reach our individual potential in life? Of course not! God is intensely interested in our personal growth and happiness. But He suggests that His followers will not pursue personal happiness as their goal. Rather, they will pursue a life of service on His behalf—motivated by the great sacrifice of Christ's life on the cross. That certainly doesn't extinguish happiness, but says that it always comes "as the unexpected surprise of a life lived in service (see Matt. 25:31-46)."[3]

"Instead of being autonomous selves 'doing our own thing,' we are called to be surrendered selves living totally under His Lordship in communities of shared life. And instead of being acquisitive selves striving and competing for our own selfish gain, God calls us to be servant selves who put the needs of others before our own (see Romans 12:10)."[4]

It is certainly true, as one Christian professor warned: "Nothing is more controversial than to be a follower of Jesus Christ. Nothing is more dangerous than to live out the will of God in today's contemporary world. It changes your whole . . . lifestyle." [5] It sure does. And it has completely changed how Seventh-day Adventists view the resources that God entrusts to each of us—we choose to be faithful, responsible stewards for God for all His resources:

Time

After God created the heavens and the earth in six literal 24-hour days, we believe that He set aside a seventh day as a weekly reminder of His creatorship (Gen. 2:1-3). He blessed it and made it holy and invited humans to come and commune with Him. Six days were given for making a living, but the seventh day He made a Sabbath day (Ex. 20:8-11).

Thus God asks of His followers one seventh of their weekly time, on Sabbath, to rejuvenate their physical and mental health, commune with Him, spend time with family and friends, and to help others.

And beyond the weekly Sabbath, God also holds all humans accountable for their use of the other six days. Time is precious. We cannot multiply it, nor retrieve it. We believe we are to use it to multiply the talents lent to us by God and to help God's cause on earth—the salvation of all who will accept it.

"The value of time is beyond computation," wrote Ellen G. White. "Christ regarded every moment as precious, and it is thus that we should regard it. Life is too short to be trifled away. We have but a few days of probation in which to prepare for eternity. We have no time to waste, no time to devote to selfish pleasures, no time for the indulgence of sin. It is now that we are to form characters for the future, immortal life. It is now that we are to prepare for the searching judgment." [6]

Thousands of things clamor for one's time. But Adventists believe that one of the highest priorities is to work as a partner with God in nurturing the spiritual lives of our families. Too many parents are ignoring this privilege, expecting it to be done by the church or school or someone else.

The Washington *Post* recently reported on a national survey that revealed a shocking portrait of how parents *don't* spend their time. "A mother on average spends 30 minutes a week in one-to-one contact with her child, and a father spends an average of 11 minutes." [7]

What in the world are they doing the rest of the week that is so important they don't have more time to spend with their children? Maybe working so hard at maintaining their place at the materialistic rat-race party.

God speaks to this hustle and bustle by providing the weekly Sabbath, and by asking His followers to simplify their lifestyles so they will have time to spiritually nurture themselves, then their families, then others, all as faithful stewards of time.

Talent

God gives special talents or abilities to every human being—from woodworking or welding skills to doing surgery or playing the violin. And the parable of the talents (Matt. 25:14-30) clearly shows that God holds every recipient responsible for the use and improvement of the talents given.

And beyond the normal or natural abilities of humans, God gives special gifts, or *spiritual* gifts, through the Holy Spirit for the building up and unifying of His church (Rom. 12:4-8; 1 Cor. 12:4-11, 27-30). "As each has received a gift," declares Peter, "employ it for one another, as good stewards of God's varied grace; . . . in order that in everything God may be glorified through Jesus Christ" (1 Peter 4:10, 11).

Physical and Mental Health

Not many years after the Seventh-day Adventist Church began, the church accepted the belief that a close relationship exists between one's physical body and spiritual life. "Do you not know," asks Paul, "that your body is a temple of the Holy Spirit within you, which you have from God? You are not your own; you were bought with a price. So glorify God in your body" (1 Cor. 6:19, 20).

With this understanding, Adventists attempt to practice good health habits that will not only protect their mind—the center of reasoning and the dwelling place of the Holy Spirit—but also keep their lives free from self-induced disease and sickness.

Seventh-day Adventists adamantly reject on biblical grounds the Greek dualism that still pervades the thinking and practice of many religions—that the physical body is a distinct, separate entity from the spiritual soul and that neither one affects the other. History plainly shows that intemperate management of one's body and mind results from such unbiblical thinking.

Adventists believe that God, as our Creator, knows better than anyone else what is best for optimum human health. Thus we attempt to follow His principles, with great emphasis upon preventive health care through the proper use of nutrition (including a balanced vegetarian diet), exercise, water, sunlight, fresh air, stimulant-free foods, rest, and trust in divine care. Indeed we are but stewards, managers, of our physical health and mind, and we choose to put into them only those things that will be consistent with Christ's life and teaching.[8] "Whatever is true, whatever is honorable, whatever is pure, . . . think about these things" (Phil. 4:8, 9).

Material Possessions

God owns everything, that is clear (Ps. 24:1). And He asks all of earth's inhabitants—not just Christians—to be managers of the goods He lends. They are given that we might multiply them and use them for His work on earth (Luke 12:13-21).

Consequently, Adventists return one tenth of their increase, as He has asked all humans to do (Mal. 3:10). It is called a tithe, or His holy tithe (Lev. 27:30-32), and is *returned,* not given, to God as our sign that all we "own" is really His.

"The gold and silver are the Lord's; and He could rain them from heaven if He chose. But instead of this He has made man His steward, entrusting him with means, not to be hoarded, but to be used in benefiting others."[9]

In addition to the tithe, Adventists freely *give* offerings out of our gratitude for the bountiful blessings that God gives to us (James 1:17).

And God's promised blessings are great for those who faithfully return tithe and give offerings: "I will . . . open the windows of heaven for you and pour down for you an overflowing blessing" (Mal. 3:10).

Adventists willingly give, for we recognize that a person's life "does not consist in the abundance of his possessions" (Luke 12:15).

Returning tithe and giving offerings, however, does not free up one to spend the remainder as selfishly as one wishes. God requires faithful stewardship over all one's possessions (Matt. 25:14-30).

And how true it is, as a Christian writer said, that "there is no room for conspicuous consumption. Our [U.S.] culture has in fact conditioned us to want more and more stuff we don't need, so that we have become consumers of God's wealth while the hungry of the world suffer and the hungry of the world die. It's time to repent of our affluence." [10]

What he is saying is that Christianity *does* make a difference in how we spend our money and how much we hoard. Just because we can't visually see any poor around us doesn't mean that we have no responsibility to help. He says that our stewardship must become global.

That means we won't spend as we wish on ourselves or even on fancy buildings, reputedly built for God but generally for our comfort and enjoyment. We believe that simplicity should mark our homes and church-owned entities so that we may share our resources with the less fortunate around the world who may not even have the simplest of shelters for a home, or a church building in which to worship, or a school to attend, or Bibles to read.

And to all of this God promises that as we give, so shall we receive: "For the measure you give will be the measure you get back" (Luke 6:38). God urges us, through the use of our resources, to lay up treasure in heaven (through faithful stewardship), "for where your treasure is, there will your heart be also" (Matt. 6:21).

Environment

From the beginning God placed humankind in charge of the earth and its resources (Gen. 1:26-28). Adam and Eve were to "subdue it," not to destroy it. Adventists strongly affirm their call to protect earth's fragile ecosphere and to speak out against the prevailing trend of "a selfish and expansionist lifestyle that exploits the poor and destroys the earth." [11]

Almost daily, pictures of pollution and a ravaged earth come to our attention—air filled with poisons, disappearing forests, beaches strewn with filth, railroad cars filled with rotting sewage, and industrial toxins escaping into the soil.

While Adventists accept the view that such destruction of the earth is a sign of the nearness of Christ's return, we do not rejoice over it but sense our responsibility to God as faithful and wise stewards of His creation—speaking out, protecting, recycling, not using products harmful to the earth, and following other earth-protective actions, as the situation demands.

Message

Paul says Christians are "servants of Christ and stewards of the mysteries of God" (1 Cor. 4:1). Indeed Christians are His ambassadors, and I believe that God has entrusted Seventh-day Adventists with a special end-time message for the world's inhabitants—the three angels' message of Revelation 14:12. We are to proclaim the everlasting gospel that calls *all* people to worship God, to keep His commandments, and to hold the faith of Jesus.

To this end we *joyfully* dedicate our time, talents, and possessions to God, for we are His stewards. And we do so in recognition of the fact that "in the gift of Jesus, God gave all heaven" for our salvation.[12]

---

* Texts quoted in this chapter are from the Revised Standard Version.

---

[1] Jon Johnston, "Growing Me-ism and Materialism," *Christianity Today Institute,* Jan. 17, 1986, p. 16.

[2] Tom Sine, *The Mustard Seed Conspiracy,* p. 78.

[3] *Ibid.*

[4] *Ibid.,* p. 83.

[5] Tony Campolo, *Adventist Review,* Apr. 20, 1989, p. 10.

[6] *Christ's Object Lessons,* p. 342.

[7] DeNeed L. Brown and Patricia Davis, "For Virginia Teens, Emptiness Amid Plenty," Washington *Post,* Dec. 8, 1991.

[8] On diet, books, alcohol, tobacco, entertainment, etc., see "Christian Behavior," *Seventh-day Adventists Believe,* pp. 272-292.

[9] *Counsels on Stewardship,* p. 15.

[10] Campolo, p. 10.

[11] Eugene Linden, *Time,* July 13, 1992, p. 68.
[12] *The Desire of Ages,* p. 565.

Associate editor of the *Adventist Review,* Myron Widmer began his service to the church in the pastoral ministry. He pastored several churches in the Pennsylvania Conference and then went to the Walla Walla College SDA Church. He holds a degree in communication from Pacific Union College and a M.Div. degree from the SDA Seminary. His hobbies include mountain hiking, gardening, and bird-watching.

Unity in the Body of Christ

*T*he church is one body with many members,
called from every nation, kindred, tongue, and
people. In Christ we are a new creation; distinc-
tions of race, culture, learning, and nationality, and differences
between high and low, rich and poor, male and female, must not
be divisive among us. We are all equal in Christ, who by one
Spirit has bonded us into one fellowship with Him and with one
another; we are to serve and be served without partiality or reservation. Through the revelation of Jesus Christ in the Scriptures
we share the same faith and hope, and reach out in one witness
to all. This unity has its source in the oneness of the triune God,
who has adopted us as His children. (Rom. 12:4, 5; 1 Cor. 12:12-
14; Matt. 28:19, 20; Ps. 133:1; 2 Cor. 5:16, 17; Acts 17:26, 27;
Gal. 3:27, 29; Col. 3:10-15; Eph. 4:14-16; John 17:20-23.)—
Fundamental Beliefs, *No. 13.*

CHAPTER THIRTEEN

By Rosa Taylor Banks

One People in Christ
The Challenge of Relationships

What a diverse family Adventists are—7 million strong internationally, with 780,000 residing in the North American Division! From a division that used to think of itself as almost entirely European in heritage, North America has become a church whose diversity reflects a mosaic of all the peoples in the world.

Roughly 59 percent of our family in North America is of Caucasian heritage—the English, German, Irish, French, Italian, Scottish, Polish, Dutch, Swedish, Norwegian, Russian, Czechoslovakian, Hungarian, Welsh, Danish, Portuguese, and other smaller ethnic groups.

Twenty-nine percent of the family consists of members of African descent—African-Americans, Bermudians, Haitians, Jamaicans, and other West Indians from the isles of the sea.

Nearly 10 percent are of Hispanic origin—Mexicans, Puerto Ricans, Cubans, Central Americans, South Americans, to name a few.

Two percent are Asian—Chinese, Filipino, Japanese, Asian-Indian, Korean, Vietnamese. And another 2 percent include other ethnic groups such as Jews, Arabs, Lebanese, Armenian, Iranian, Syrian, and native people.

Nearly 62 percent of the North American family consists of women; about 25 percent are youth; 15 percent are the elderly; and approximately 12 percent are disabled.

In addition to the major languages we speak, such as English, Spanish, French, and German, our multicultural family speaks approximately 40 tongues and dialects. The North American Division of Seventh-day Adventists weaves a rich tapestry of diversity. Its rich mix of race, nationality, culture, age, gender, abilities, handicaps, impairments, attitudes, and thoughts is the result of witnessing in the midst of a broken world that is fractured into many diverse groups. Its members are brought into its fellowship, where they become transformed into a new people, a new community, and a new society based on love and peace.

We must applaud ourselves for this diversity because it means that Adventists have faithfully responded to the gospel commission, at least in part. The tremendous challenge is how to take this diverse membership and transform it into one great community of love.

Let's Include Everybody

Will our church in North America and worldwide use its wonderful mosaic of difference to create a truly pluralistic denomination? Will it take positive and rapid steps to remove all the barriers so that those who have been traditionally underrepresented and underutilized will be given equal opportunity to develop and use their skills fully for the church? The future of our church depends on affirmative answers to these questions. We also need definite strategies that will identify all the barriers to successful bridge building; for if our problems are not brought out into the open, we may never admit that problems do exist. The commonly repeated axiom "If it's not broken, don't fix it" comes into play when an organization sticks its head in the sand on apparent issues.

Clearly, we must find ways to maintain social stability and internal cohesion as our constituency becomes more and more racially and culturally heterogeneous. It is no longer good enough for our church to promote its human relations policies and maintain statistics on its ethnic cultures as badges of commitment to promoting unity as a priority. Policies alone cannot affirm diversity and bring about radical changes in a church that is expected to model "oneness."

To achieve the goal of oneness, love for each other must emanate from the heart. Only when the heart is changed will

110

deterrents to unity disappear and the church become the witness that Christ desires it to become. That is the reason we must come to grips with our problems in this generation. We cannot replace human rights with racial fears and stereotypes. We cannot close our eyes to even small occurrences of discrimination in the church and hope they will disappear. They will continue to exist among us, and haunt us, too, unless we address them openly and make unity a priority.

I am particularly interested in our addressing these deterrents that mitigate against improved human relationships and the ideal of oneness—deterrents such as racism, discrimination, stereotyping, and the like. I believe that the nineties call for tremendous change in our beliefs and attitudes. The nineties challenge us to shape a future of unity and oneness by making this theme the priority it should be. A future that includes an acceptance of each person as a "brother" or "sister" in Christ and each culture as being essential and significant to the whole will not automatically happen, even in the remnant church. We ourselves, empowered by the Spirit, must create it by what we do. By the grace of God, we are the ones who must make what tomorrow will be like for our church, and we must begin doing that today!

Jesus supports this view in the prayer of His Father. "As thou hast sent me into the world, even so have I also sent them into the world. And for their sakes I sanctify myself, that they also might be sanctified through the truth. Neither pray I for these alone, but for them also which shall believe on me through their word; that they all may be one; as thou, Father, art in me, and I in thee, that they also may be one in us: that the world may believe that thou hast sent me" (John 17:18-21).

The Christian view of unity holds that there must be for Christians a spirit of cohesion for which the world at large is not ready, a unity that is ultimate and indivisible, a bond stronger than that of biological kinship. The ethnic problem within our Christian fellowship should be resolved not only through our awareness of our biological identity, but in that oneness that Christians have in Christ, not after the flesh but after the Spirit, not in the solid and shared flesh of humanity, but in the broken and shared body of Christ. We are not merely members of one

111

flesh, but members of that one body. We have our oneness not alone in the common blood of our physical life, but in our oneness in Christ Jesus.

If the world is placing barriers before any of its ethnic groups, then in this spirit of love, the church should be visibly removing them. If the world regards certain ethnic characteristics as negative, the church should seek to dispel these stereotypes and negative connotations aimed at members of a microculture.

If our society knowingly or unknowingly builds walls to separate the races, then the church must build bridges of unity. That is what the Master meant when He continued His prayer to His Father, "I in them, and thou in me, that they may be made perfect in one; and that the world may know that thou hast sent me, and hast loved them" (verse 23). Herein is our model of oneness.

The Great Commission requires that we go into all the world and preach the gospel (Matt. 28:18-20). The response of races, cultures, and nations of the world to the gospel presents us with at least four challenges if we are to make progress in this era as a church that takes advantage of the windows of opportunity and uses them to mirror Jesus more visibly.

1. The Challenge of Affirming Diversity

We must acknowledge that the differences among races, nations, cultures, and their various histories are at least as profound and as durable as the similarities, and that these differences are not divagations from European norm, but structures eminently worth knowing about for their sake. Members have to know that if we cannot navigate difference, we can never achieve unity in the body of Christ.

We are challenged to engage in the exciting adventure of modeling God's future for our church in harmony with His purpose for all creation—that we "are all one in Christ Jesus" (Gal. 3:28). We must work for the fulfillment of God's purpose in human history and its natural context and environment. This is a vision the church must possess if it is to become a part of God's new creation.

2. The Challenge of a Higher Law

We must develop in and among God's people a spirit that will enable them to transcend their ethnic, cultural, and physiological differences, likes, and dislikes; and to become willingly obedient to unenforceable obligations that are beyond the reach of the policies of the church or the laws of society. These concern inner attitudes, expressions, and compassions that policies cannot regulate and discipline cannot rectify. Such obligations are met by an inner higher law written in our hearts that produces love. Human problems cannot be solved without the spirit of love and brotherhood. Love is still our most potent weapon for personal and social transformation.

3. The Challenge of Enlightenment

Jesus prayed, "Father, forgive them; for they know not what they do" (Luke 23:34). Some of the most inexpressible tragedies of history are performed by people who "know not what they do." Men like Abraham Lincoln, John F. Kennedy, Martin Luther King, Jr., and Robert F. Kennedy were assassinated by people steeped in blindness, people devoid of integrity, people who were misguided. Prejudice, hatred, and stereotyping are examples of human blindness, wherever practiced and in whatever form.

Our church has a mandate to avoid intellectual and moral blindness, and to conquer both sin and ignorance wherever they occur within the fellowship. It also has a moral obligation to correct any injustices that may be found, and to provide equal opportunity to any group that has been formerly underrepresented or whose skills have been underutilized.

4. The Challenge of Creativity

Farsightedness, courage, vision are all essential for developing new approaches to human relations problem solving. What we need is not a greater escalation of conflicts but an effort on the part of both sides to improve the quality and structure of discussion. We need to raise the level of understanding regarding the nature of conflicts and the parties involved. New approaches to decision making are also needed in which professional laypersons in fields such as psychology and human services can play a significant role. This will call for discarding old leadership styles that don't work anymore and employing strategies that do;

113

and having the wisdom to know the difference between the two.

In short, we are challenged to meet the needs of our diverse membership by developing an appreciation for other cultures and by building bridges that cross racial and ethnic lines. In the nineties we cannot wait for society to lead the way. We must launch an offensive against division and disunity, just as we do against sin and worldliness.

Division Versus Unity

The two major powers in the world, hatred and love, are synonymous with division and unity. As such, they remind us of two occurrences in the Bible: Babel (Gen. 11:1-9) and Pentecost (Acts 2:1-13). The Tower of Babel resembles division and discord, while the Pentecostal experience is one of unity and love. Wherever we find members revealing the brokenness of our contemporary society, we can be certain that those members are still at the Tower of Babel in their spiritual lives.

The church should thank God that there is also Pentecost, and that each of us can experience it in our own lives, starting right now. When Pentecost takes place in the church, the power of God's Spirit breaches the walls of partition, and the church is given to the world as God's new creation. The church then becomes a community in which barriers of language, nation, race, culture, gender, and physical handicap are overcome; for the Spirit of God makes one new humanity in Jesus Christ.

Ellen White adds clarity to the subject: "No distinction on account of nationality, race, or caste is recognized by God. He is the Maker of all mankind. All men are of one family by creation, and all are one through redemption. Jesus came to demolish every wall of partition, to throw open every compartment of the temple, that every soul may have free access to God" (*Christ's Object Lessons,* p. 386).

She further states: "Christ came to this earth with a message of mercy and forgiveness. He laid the foundation for a religion by which Jew and Gentile, black and white, free and bond, are linked together in one common brotherhood, recognized as equal in the sight of God. The Saviour has a boundless love for every human being. In each one He sees capacity for improvement. With divine

114

energy and hope He greets those for whom He has given His life. In His strength they can live a life rich in good works, filled with the power of the Spirit" (*Testimonies,* vol. 7, p. 225).

Our church has to come to terms with diversity. Because of Pentecost, our church has to affirm diversity as well as celebrate it. To achieve its goal of harmony, it must provide education and training opportunities for its membership and work force. It must also encourage cross-cultural experiences and even structure some programs to get us started in that direction. And whenever frictions occur, they must be resolved in ways that bring about reconciliation among the races and cultures. Why? That we might continue to grow in grace and love and peace. Why? "That we may all be one, and that the world may believe that God sent Jesus and Jesus sent us into the world" (see John 17:22, 23, 28).

Today, more than ever, we are learning in North America that no one culture holds a corner on knowledge, but that we must learn from each other in order to broaden each other's understanding of the universe. And we must learn these lessons on this side of the kingdom, or we will feel uncomfortable standing in the presence of that large multiracial body that will be gathered around the throne.

Rosa Banks has an Ed.D. & L.H.D. in business and higher education administration and has the distinction of being the first woman vice president of Oakwood College. She is also the first female associate secretary of the North American Division. Currently Banks serves the NAD as associate secretary and director of the Office of Human Relations. Her household includes her husband, Halsey Banks, two children, and a nephew.

The Remnant and Its Mission

*T*he universal church is composed of all who truly believe in Christ, but in the last days, a time of widespread apostasy, a remnant has been called out to keep the commandments of God and the faith of Jesus. This remnant announces the arrival of the judgment hour, proclaims salvation through Christ, and heralds the approach of His second advent. This proclamation is symbolized by the three angels of Revelation 14; it coincides with the work of judgment in heaven and results in a work of repentance and reform on earth. Every believer is called to have a personal part in this worldwide witness. (Rev. 12:17; 14:6-12; 18:1-4; 2 Cor. 5:10; Jude 3, 14; 1 Peter 1:16-19; 2 Peter 3:10-14; Rev. 21:1-14.)—Fundamental Beliefs, *No. 12.*

CHAPTER FOURTEEN

By Tom Shepherd

Alarming Good News
The Three Angels' Messages for the Nineties

I was a student colporteur one summer in the early 1970s. Our student leader, Bill, was enthusiastic and fun to be with. He talked about witnessing and said we should remember to talk about the "three C's"—Christ, the cross, and the (Second) Coming. "But avoid the 'three M's,'" he continued—"meat, millennium, and the mark of the beast."

Perhaps the three angels' messages have that ring of three M's to some—sort of a backwater of Adventism, funny beasts and charts and a big tent with sawdust on the floor. Quaint, a nice logo, but not very important for the 1990s. The surprise, on close examination, is that these three messages are very pertinent to us today. But to catch the vista they present, we have to overcome our reluctance to wade into the dazzling symbols and themes of Revelation.

Jesus in the Center

The three angels actually form part of a series of seven angels in Revelation 14. The first three angels proclaim the three messages of Revelation 14:6-12. These are paralleled by three others in Revelation 14:15-20, the second trio completing in action what the first three angels proclaimed in word.[1] At the center of the drama is the seventh "angel," the Son of man, on clouds of glory (Rev. 14:14). The context thus leads us to our first conclusion: Jesus Christ and His return are the goal and fruition of the three angels' messages.

Seeing the pattern of seven angels highlights the significance

117

of the three messages. But another key to their interpretation opens the door wider: the numerous allusions in Revelation to Old Testament passages. With careful analysis we can often pinpoint which Old Testament references the apostle had in mind when writing.[2] These can throw enormous light on the message of Revelation.

The first angel (Rev. 14:6, 7) brings the gospel: "Then I saw another angel flying in midair, and he had the eternal gospel to proclaim to those who live on the earth—to every nation, tribe, language and people. He said in a loud voice, 'Fear God and give him glory, because the hour of his judgment has come. Worship him who made the heavens, the earth, the sea and the springs of water.' " *

The words here may not sound like "righteousness by faith" and "saved by grace," which we so often link with the good news, but the angel's words do hold a striking resemblance to the preaching of Jesus.

Jesus said, "The time has come. . . . The kingdom of God is near. Repent and believe the good news!" (Mark 1:15). His reference to *time* parallels the first angel's reference to the *hour* of judgment. The *kingdom of God* matches the *judgment,* which turns the kingdom over to God's people.[3] The call to *repentance and belief* coincides with the call to *fear, glorify, and worship God.* The gospel in Revelation 14 is "everlasting," rooted in the preaching of Jesus Himself. The last-day people of God proclaim the message of Jesus expressed in its harvest-day setting.

Understanding the First Message

What does it mean to fear, glorify, and worship God? The likely Old Testament passages standing behind this angel's message are Jeremiah 10 (see sidebar); Psalms 86 and 111; Deuteronomy 32:34-43; Daniel 7; and Exodus 20:8-11. These passages emphasize four major themes: (1) the insignificance and inadequacy of idols in comparison with the Creator, (2) God's righteous judgment against evil, (3) the Sabbath as a sign of God's creatorship, and (4) the glory of God revealed in mighty acts of redemption for His people. You have to read the passages to get their spirit, a sense of the power and control of God over creation, and His wonderful mercy in coming to the aid of His people.

At the heart of these passages are two pictures of God—Creator and Redeemer. His role as Creator provides the ground for our worship.[4] His role as Redeemer is expressed in judgment, a judgment that punishes wickedness and saves His people from certain death.

The Scriptures provide another picture of the terms "fear God" and "give glory to God." The fear of the Lord is hailed throughout the Old Testament. It finds its root conception in the relation of the creature to the Creator. We are to live in His presence in recognition of who He is. We err in jumping too quickly from the term *fear* to the softer term *reverence*. The "fear of the Lord" most certainly includes reverence, but an examination of Old Testament appearances of God indicates that when He appears people tremble. This, however, is not only an Old Testament phenomenon. The same holds true in the New Testament.[5]

Clear Consequences

This has clear consequences for our daily lives. The use of "fear God" and similar terminology in Leviticus 19 illustrates the point. "Do not curse the deaf or put a stumbling block in front of the blind, but fear your God. I am the Lord" (Lev. 19:14). Our relation to God controls our relation to the rest of creation. To love God means we must show love to others. We must give ourselves in acts of grace and mercy, caring for people and respecting all life and creation. The first angel demands it. To claim this message as ours and yet to do otherwise is hypocrisy, telling a lie.

And the first angel is against lies. The solemn words "give glory to God" are an Old Testament oath for truth-telling. When wicked Achan was brought before Joshua, the distinguished leader proclaimed, "My son, give glory to the Lord, the God of Israel, and give him the praise. Tell me what you have done; do not hide it from me" (Joshua 7:19).

The same idiom reappears in John 9:24, where the Jewish leaders call upon the man born blind to tell the truth about his healing. In Revelation the beasts of chapter 13 and their followers tell lies about God and His people. The angel warns that this must change.

The message does not slacken its hammer blows. Living the truth is set in the context of the judgment of God. Here Daniel 7 is the clear Old Testament passage in view.[6] This judgment that "has come" precedes the Second Advent (Rev. 14:14-20).

It is easy to procrastinate in life's most earnest issues. We count their value often when opportunities to fulfill them have slipped through our fingers. But a deadline focuses the mind. And God's judgment is such a deadline. If you have ever missed a plane or an important appointment, you know that sinking feeling in your *heart*. But to "miss" God's judgment, to fall short, to be locked outside the Bridegroom's house, puts a sinking feeling in the *soul*.

God's Final Appeals

The second and third angels' messages are a foretaste of that bitter experience. They are, in fact, the deepest of appeals to a world gone awry. The principal issue over which these angels send their trumpet calls is *worship*, a worship centered in an image rather than the Creator-God (see Rev. 13).

The central Old Testament passages behind these two messages are Isaiah 21 and 34; Jeremiah 25 and 50, 51; Ezekiel 9; Daniel 5; Genesis 19; and 2 Kings 1. Space does not permit a review of all of these passages. Read them and catch their thrust.

If there is anything that the Scriptures repeat again and again, it is God's hatred of idols and His love for His people. While the second and third angels' messages foretell doom to the rejecters of God, they also proclaim liberty to God's persecuted people. Babylon's fall (the second message) is good news to the people of God oppressed by an idol-making power (Rev. 13). The fall of evil is the dawn of peace.[7]

But by far, these last two messages are a striking warning to those enamored with evil. The sobering words of the prophet Daniel to Belshazzar expose the central problem. After retelling the experience of Nebuchadnezzar, the prophet continues: "But you his son, O Belshazzar, have not humbled yourself, though you knew all this. Instead, you have set yourself up against the Lord of heaven. . . . You praised the gods of silver and gold, of bronze, iron, wood and stone, which cannot see or hear or understand. But you did not honor the God who holds in his hand your life and all your ways" (Dan. 5:22, 23).

When you "set yourself up against the Lord of heaven," you cannot honor (fear/worship) Him. The center of sin has always been "I." And the setting up of this type of idol invariably has resulted in unethical behavior toward others. We become like that which we adore: lifeless, unfeeling, hard—like the idols we worship. This has been the world's problem from the beginning in Eden. It is still the problem of the nineties.

"Though you knew all this," the prophet said to the impious king. That's the rub. To make an error unknowingly is one thing, but to flaunt blasphemy invites righteous judgment. The third angel's message rings with wrath. But is this compatible with God's nature of love? How can "tormented with burning sulfur" (Rev. 14:10) be part of the good news?

Difficult questions. Sometimes the solution sought is a refashioning or reinterpreting of the ancient message to "speak" (as we say) to modern people. I fear that we lose much by such "retelling." In reinterpreting the ancient message we can mute its critique of our own world. We do well to allow the dissonance of the ancient text to rest on our hearts until a deeper message from God rings in our souls.

What Kind of God Is This?

The Scriptures make it plain that God desires the death of no one.[8] The blame for the eternal death of the sinner cannot be laid at nail-scarred feet. Christ bore that eternal death once for all (Heb. 9:26-28). Thus, those who are lost carry their own guilt and blame into the eternal silence. That is the heaviest punishment.

And yet we must face the accusation made by some that we serve a God who says, "Love Me or I'll kill you." The problem with this viewpoint is that it takes only the Godward side of life's equation into consideration, as though there were some neutral ground one could occupy to judge God. The Bible indicates a rather different scene—a world (and each one of us!) lost, desolate in sin, in slavery to an evil power none of us is capable of resisting.[9]

Into our hopeless situation (we are much like the servant who owed 10,000 talents in Matthew 18) God injects an amazing offer of *mercy*. The humanward side of life's equation is the question of how we will respond to the mercy of God. The servant in the parable responded by despising the grace of the master.

Despise Grace

What does it mean to despise grace? It means to accept it as *our due,* something owed to us and, therefore, without necessity of our response. To act in this way toward grace results in *no change in the life*.

The dire consequences of such a distortion of reality are depicted in the master's response in the parable. The servant is denoted as "wicked." The same picture shows up in Revelation 13 and 14, where the worshipers of the beast consider their persecution of the saints an appropriate action. However, the judgment of God brings all this to nought by bringing reality crashing down on the heads of those who dare to touch His own.

The three angels' messages—fresh and lively—spark with the issues of today and dazzle in the scope of their vision. They are insistent with appeals to a world on the brink of disaster. It was not by accident that our early pioneers embraced them as the vision of our movement. These messages set the sails for the kingdom of God. Their clarion call proclaims the good news of the Creator-Redeemer. And they appeal to us to flee the terrible danger of worshiping anyone but God alone.

I find the three angels' messages full of grace. They provide me a personal vision for life, a goal in serving my Lord—for taking the good news to all the world. I thank God for the three angels' messages.

---

*All Scripture references in this chapter are from the New International Version.

---

[1] A careful comparison of the wording of Revelation 14:15-20 with 14:6-12 shows how each of the last three angels parallels the first three. Note the parallel uses of the words "another" and "loud voice" in the two passages and observe how the messages match the outcomes.

[2] Dr. Jon Paulien of Andrews University, in his book *Decoding Revelation's*

Trumpets (Berrien Springs, Mich.: Andrews University Press, 1987), illustrates a method to determine which Old Testament passages stand behind a text in Revelation: (1) look for parallel passages in Revelation itself and check for clear Old Testament allusions to these; (2) note key terms, especially rare ones, in the text of Revelation that show up in the Old Testament text alluded to, and (3) note patterns of telling the story in Revelation that may echo a similar pattern in the Old Testament passage alluded to.

The three angels' messages find numerous parallels in the rest of Revelation: Revelation 14:15-20, already noted, is one. The first angel is paralleled in 15:1-4 (cf. Rev. 16:5-7), the second angel in Revelation 18:1-8, and the third angel in Revelation 19:11-20:15. With the help of these other parallels, it is easier to pinpoint Old Testament backgrounds to the three angels' messages.

[3] Compare the judgment scene in Daniel 7, which has clear links to Revelation 13 and 14.

[4] The connection with the Sabbath commandment is clear. Our observance of the Sabbath is a sign of allegiance to the Creator. In Revelation 13 the evil beasts demand worship of an idol. Refusal to obey means certain death (a clear allusion to Daniel 3). Such stark realities focus the mind and reveal the heart. We can serve either God or the beast, not both.

[5] See, for instance, the theophany at the Mount of Transfiguration, Matthew 17:1-8; Mark 9:2-8; Luke 9:28-36.

[6] The broad context of Revelation 13 and 14 points in this direction. The beast powers of Revelation 13 and the mention of the 1260-day prophecy clearly point to Daniel 7.

[7] Cf. Isaiah 34:8, where God's retribution upholds Zion's cause.

[8] See Ezekiel 18:30-32, 2 Peter 3:9, and Revelation 3:20, 21.

[9] See Romans 1-3 and 7:14-25, for examples.

After graduating with a degree in theology from Pacific Union College, Tom Shepherd studied public health at Loma Linda University and then served as a minister in the Illinois Conference. Next he and his wife served as medical missionaries in the African country of Malawi. While Sherry, his wife, worked in the Adventist health centre in Blantyre, he administered rural clinics and ADRA development. Returning to the United States, he completed M.A. and Ph.D. degrees in New Testament at Andrews University. Currently he is professor of New Testament at Brazil Adventist College.

The Life, Death, and Resurrection of Christ

*I*n Christ's life of perfect obedience to God's will, His suffering, death, and resurrection, God provided the only means of atonement for human sin, so that those who by faith accept this atonement may have eternal life, and the whole creation may better understand the infinite and holy love of the Creator. This perfect atonement vindicates the righteousness of God's law and the graciousness of His character; for it both condemns our sin and provides for our forgiveness. The death of Christ is substitutionary and expiatory, reconciling and transforming. The resurrection of Christ proclaims God's triumph over the forces of evil, and for those who accept the atonement assures their final victory over sin and death. It declares the Lordship of Jesus Christ, before whom every knee in heaven and on earth will bow. (John 3:16; Isa. 53; 1 Peter 2:21, 22; 1 Cor. 15:3, 4, 20-22; 2 Cor. 5:14, 15, 19-21; Rom. 1:4; 3:25; 4:25; 8:3, 4; 1 John 2:2; 4:10; Col. 2:15; Phil. 2:6-11.)—Fundamental Beliefs, *No. 9.*

CHAPTER FIFTEEN

By George W. Reid

Why Did Jesus Die?
How God Saves Us

With the end of the first century of the Christian Era and the death of John—the last intimate eyewitness of Christ's ministry—questions previously taken for granted began to surface: Who was Jesus? Why did He come? Why did He die?

Responses to such queries came through a host of metaphors found in the Scriptures: the sacrificial Lamb of God that taketh away the sins of the world; the conquering King of kings; the Light of the world. Jesus was seen as the Son of God—a cosmic deliverer, an emissary from heaven. But also as the Son of man, identifying with us.

One of the most telling pictures lies in the idea of ransom. Jesus says: "The Son of man came not to be served but to serve, and to give his life as a ransom for many" (Matt. 20:28).* And echoing Him, Peter says: "You know that you were ransomed from the futile ways inherited from your fathers, not with perishable things such as silver or gold, but with the precious blood of Christ, like that of a lamb without blemish or spot" (1 Peter 1:18, 19).

The idea of ransom was common in the ancient world. The word indicated something of value used to reclaim something from a pawnshop. It also referred to the purchase of freedom by a slave. Of course, the ancients also knew all too well about the practice of paying ransom for release of a captured hostage or prisoner of war. Hence Paul's comment: "You were bought with a price; do not become slaves of men" (1 Cor. 7:23).

125

The Ransom Price

However, restless imaginations soon went to work, and raised the question: If ransomed, who collected the ransom price?

Interestingly, the Bible never says. Over the centuries a dramatic scenario took shape—part fact, part fiction. According to the tale, a deal was struck between the Father and Satan. Adam had sold his rights—indeed, his soul—to the devil. Knowing the Father's earnest desire to have Adam returned, Satan, with a fiendish cackle, demanded the ultimate price: the life of the Son of God, the final object of Lucifer's hatred.

So Jesus came—so goes the scenario—and lived under the duress of Satan's torment, and finally forfeited His life. But according to the story, Lucifer himself was fooled, for the Father raised His Son from the grave, leaving Lucifer shorn of his prize, possessor of nothing but an empty tomb. He lost the prize he had extorted from the Father.

The Important Truth

Despite the fantasy window dressing, we discover here a nugget of truth. Christ did indeed give His life a ransom for us sinners. But the worthwhile question has little to do with who received payment. There is a far more important truth—namely, that in Christ's atonement a monumental price was paid, not in crass commercial terms, but to accomplish reconciliation between us as fallen sinners and our righteous God, to set us right with God. "For if while we were enemies we were reconciled to God by the death of his Son, much more, now that we are reconciled, shall we be saved by his life" (Rom. 5:10).

Before a watching universe God demonstrated once for all how far He would go to make possible redemption of lost sinners. In this extension of His love is revealed the manner in which His sacrifice partakes of ransom qualities.

We must never forget that it was our God who initiated our rescue, who reached out to us. "All this is from God, who through Christ reconciled us to himself" (2 Cor. 5:18). And He continues to reach out to us today. When we accept His merciful invitation, we walk in the certainty of salvation guaranteed by His death and resurrection.

WHY DID JESUS DIE?

In one brief sentence Paul probes the depths of what it means for God to love. "But God shows his love for us in that while we were yet sinners Christ died for us" (Rom. 5:8).

Three truths leap out at us. First, God demonstrates His kind of love. Second, we grasp our helpless, ever-ignorant condition as sinners. And third, we watch Him initiate the whole plan.

In God's plan Christ fulfills the everlasting covenant, meeting a commitment crafted before the world was. He would volunteer to lay down His life for us. As Adventists understand especially well, He was fulfilling concurrently a purpose of cosmic proportions.

But what about His love?

Unfortunately, love has become an almost shapeless word. Often it is tied to sentiment, and even confused with a religious feeling. But as used in the Bible, love is a power word, not a soft fuzzy. Love is aggressive: God at work tracking us down to help us. Love is a principle, Ellen White says. How can that be? The answer is that God's love is an unshakable commitment, inviolable, a predisposition in our favor that cannot be discouraged. Divine love—there is no way to shake it or deter it. It is a relentless pursuit by a God eager to help, one who never gives up. In this sense God is love.

More Than Example

In the high Middle Ages a French monk, Peter Abelard, constructed what he felt described what love really means. It has come to be called the moral influence theory. Reacting against the coarse ransom idea of his time, he argued that in no sense was Jesus a ransom, but someone elevated. If only we could grasp the nobility of God's character, he reasoned, our self-ridden hearts would melt and be moved to repentance, and sin would be abandoned.

For Abelard, Christ's death really was the ultimate demonstration of God's love, hence a description of His character. So Jesus suffered with us to set the example. He identified fully and tasted all of life. He suffered *with* the sinner rather than directly *for* the sinner. This theory reinterpreted the meaning of those texts that tell us Christ died for us.

Despite its core truth, Abelard's doctrine fell far short of the

127

full biblical picture. It presents Christ as subject to the law of love rather than being its Creator. Its soft view of sin suggests that difficulty arises not so much from the sinner's violation of God's perfect character as from his failure to understand God's affection for him. It leaves to wander the biblical teaching that Christ came not only to demonstrate God's love but to manifest His justice as well. With the atonement described principally in terms of enlightening us about His purpose, Christ's work as a sacrifice dying for guilty sinners is muted. The focus falls especially on inward moral enlightenment, not so much on a plain and open outward death that resolved the major conflict sin had introduced in God's universe. So Abelard brought us a partial truth—Jesus as the demonstration beyond all question of God's unfailing concern for us.

But salvation means more than good feeling between us and God. It means a grueling confrontation between righteousness and human revolt that entangles us all. It means a love that carried Jesus to the ultimate sacrifice to obtain for us reconciliation with our Creator. The ghastly physical scene at Golgotha spoke only dimly to humans of a kind of love that, in fact, means taking up the guilt of every sin and bearing its consequence: total alienation from God. Only here surfaces the depths of God's self-sacrificing, persistent love.

So, as Paul says, "we have peace with God through our Lord Jesus Christ" (verse 1). We have the joy of certain salvation as we accept Him, knowing ourselves fully accepted in His love. God is love, and the magnitude of that love will continue to unfold before us as we stride through the gates into eternity.

Tucked away in a familiar New Testament text is a truth usually obscured by translators. "They are justified by his grace as a gift, through the redemption which is in Christ Jesus, whom God put forward as an expiation by his blood, to be received by faith" (Rom. 3:24, 25). Literally the text says Christ became our place of sacrifice (Greek, *hilasterion*), an unclouded reference to the ancient Hebrew sacrificial system. Both on the surface and at bedrock, the principle is substitution.

Typical of pagan religions, the ancient Greeks worked to appease their gods, quieting the gods' anger and seeking favor with gifts and a regimen of specified deeds. Unfortunately, this concept persists among some Christians today, at times surfacing in arguments over faith and works. But appeasement on any grounds is a pagan idea worthy of rejection.

The Father's Favor

In Christ's death is no hint of the Saviour's effort to win the favor of the Father. With that favor already in hand, His confidence carried Him to Calvary, despite a shuddering of His human frame. Only on the cross, confronted by withdrawal of His Father's presence in revulsion against sin, did the stark break become clear. As the veil of our guilt fell over Him, there was expressed from His lips an agonizing cry, "Why hast thou forsaken me?" (Matt. 27:46).

With this He slipped into the pit of the second death, carrying the burden of rejection for rebellion against God. At that point He is in our place. His is the despair of lost sinners staring into a black hole of oblivion, devoid of hope. Standing in our place, "The Saviour could not see through the portals of the tomb" *(The Desire of Ages,* p. 753). Death overtook Him as the abandoned sinner, alone, in the place where each of us really belongs.

Some suggest that Christ came primarily to show His concern for us in our common human fate, to share our sorrows, to assure us God understands and cares. While all this has merit, it carries the subtle suggestion that, after all, sin is not really that serious and we should take final comfort in the knowledge that God never ceases caring. We are encouraged to look on the sunny side. But what sunlight ever falls on the precipice overlooking doom? Beyond question, Jesus demonstrates how God loves, but much more was at stake. He came to bear the inevitable punishment for revolt against the infinitely righteous character of God.

Jesus came, not to appease, but to cancel guilt and cleanse sinners. In no sense is this bribery of God or adroit footwork to meet some sort of personal demand. Instead, it was a calculated divine plan of which Paul said: "This was to show God's righteousness, because in his divine forbearance he had passed over former sins; it was to prove at the present time that he himself is righteous and that he justifies him who has faith in Jesus" (Rom.

3:25, 26). *In other words, rather than responding to God's demand, it was done at God's initiative.*

Along the way Jesus paid our ransom and freed us, the captives of sin. Along the way He showed how God loves. But there is much more. Real understanding comes when we come to grips with the desperate nature of our sin problem and how God must deal with rebellion running loose in His universe.

At question is God's righteousness, His justness. Here is a dramatic departure from pagan ideas of appeasement. God undertakes to bridge the gulf. He substitutes Himself to demonstrate the changeless nature of His law, and performs all that's needed. Christ becomes the divine sacrifice, His cross an altar (see 1 Cor. 5:7). In amazement we stand aside, watching as He takes it up in our behalf. He "gave himself up for us" (Eph. 5:2) and "offered for all time a single sacrifice for sins" (Heb. 10:12). God "sent his Son to be the expiation for our sins" (1 John 4:10).

In Christ our sin was judged and condemned. God's righteous nature remains intact and its violation dispatched. While we stood like wide-eyed children, He reconciled us, now to shower the benefits upon us who accept Him in faith. With the universe as witness to it all, what more could He do?

---

* All Bible references in this chapter are taken from the Revised Standard Version.

George W. Reid has been a pastor, an evangelist, a teacher, an editor, and a church administrator. Currently he is a general field secretary of the General Conference of Seventh-day Adventists and director of the Biblical Research Institute. He authored *A Sound of Trumpets: Americans, Adventists, and Health Reform* and holds degrees from Union College, the SDA Theological Seminary, and Southwestern Baptist Theological Seminary. He has two grown children.

Christian Behavior

We are called to be a godly people who think, feel, and act in harmony with the principles of heaven. For the Spirit to recreate in us the character of our Lord we involve ourselves only in those things which will produce Christlike purity, health, and joy in our lives. This means that our amusement and entertainment should meet the highest standards of Christian taste and beauty. While recognizing cultural differences, our dress is to be simple, modest, and neat, befitting those whose true beauty does not consist of outward adornment but in the imperishable ornament of a gentle and quiet spirit. It also means that because our bodies are the temples of the Holy Spirit, we are to care for them intelligently. Along with adequate exercise and rest, we are to adopt the most healthful diet possible and abstain from the unclean foods identified in the Scriptures. Since alcoholic beverages, tobacco, and the irresponsible use of drugs and narcotics are harmful to our bodies, we are to abstain from them as well. Instead, we are to engage in whatever brings our thoughts and bodies into the discipline of Christ, who desires our wholesomeness, joy, and goodness. (Rom. 12:1, 2; 1 John 2:6; Eph. 5:1-21; Phil. 4:8; 2 Cor. 10:5; 6:14-7:1; 1 Peter 3:1-4; 1 Cor. 6:10, 20; 10:31; Lev. 11:1-47; 3 John 2.)—Fundamental Beliefs, No. 21.

CHAPTER SIXTEEN

By *Jay Gallimore*

Christian Standards
Minimums, Not Maximums

W hat should be our attitude toward lifestyle instructions? Does the church have the authority to tell us how we should conduct our lives in an evil society? Are guidelines on behavior relics of the eighteenth century that mature Christians don't need—or worse, legalism? Did the New Testament church simply introduce people to Jesus and then leave them on their own?

Some Adventists may be surprised to discover that the early church actually enjoined lifestyle conformity in certain areas. While we probably don't have a record of all they addressed, we do have a model of how they settled issues. Refusing to leave each congregation or territory to settle disputes, they gathered in Jerusalem through a delegated representation (Acts 15:2).

One of the first lifestyle issues concerned the eating of food offered to idols. While not a problem in most Western societies today, it was a burning issue in the early church. Many felt such a prohibition was irrelevant, out of touch, and inconvenient. Why should leaders make all the fuss about eating such food when it had no effect on their relationship with the Lord? Up to that time, eating food offered to idols seems not to have been an issue, although in the Old Testament God had referred to the practice as playing the harlot after other gods (Ex. 34:15).

The Jerusalem Council took a clear stand. Its official letter, sent out to the Gentile believers through the hands of Judas Barsabbas and Silas, stated: "You are to abstain from food sacrificed to idols" (Acts 15:22, 29, NIV).

But the matter didn't end there. Feelings became so intense as to threaten not only the unity of the church but the very faith of its Gentile believers. Jewish converts living outside Palestine opposed the Jerusalem prohibition, bringing to bear convincing arguments. Paul had to face this problem. In 1 Corinthians 8 he agrees with their reasoning, affirming that those who say that eating idol food doesn't affect their walk with God have a good point. Like most of them, he grew up believing that an idol was nothing. He had no spiritual or emotional ties to such lifeless objects. In his understanding, eating food offered to nothing amounted to nothing.

Yet when these Christians were ready to tell the leaders at Jerusalem to mind their own business, Paul tells them, "Knowledge puffs up, but love builds up" (1 Cor. 8:1, NIV). Kindly but firmly he points out to these intelligent believers that they had missed the point. While not mentioning the Jerusalem Council by name, he defends its command with a powerful appeal that should shape our attitudes about church standards today.

Paul and the Jerusalem Council knew the Gentile converts had been used to eating food offered to idols as an act of worship. This made them vulnerable to backsliding. Further, in many of the cities of the Roman Empire Christians had a difficult time finding food that had not been first offered to an idol. A scenario like the following could have become all too common: When Brother and Sister Gentile arrived at fellowship lunch and discovered Brother and Sister Jew eating idol food, they were confused. Brother and Sister Jew gave them their rationale and convinced them that it didn't matter. Unknown to Brother and Sister Jew, the Gentile family went home and accepted an invitation to visit Mr. and Mrs. Pagan's home. In the process, they were given more food that had been offered to an idol. After a few more social occasions, Brother and Sister Gentile were swept back into their idol worship.

No doubt this practice also tempted many borderline Jews. Even for strong Jews, the allurements of a foreign environment could not be discounted. Paul urges the early Christians to take care lest their "liberty" become a "stumbling block" to their brothers (1 Cor. 8:9, NIV). Earlier Jesus had solemnly warned that it would be better to be drowned than to be a stumbling block and face the day of judgment (Matt. 18:6).

How does one become a stumbling block? When Jesus raised the issue of stumbling blocks, He spoke to the church as a community. Likewise Paul warns that those who follow their own "knowledge" instead of obeying the prohibition will become a "stumbling block" (1 Cor. 8:9, 13, NASB). We may conclude that when a person ignores or flaunts what the church has agreed to, his or her practice not only tempts a fellow believer but destroys the unity and harmony of the church.

Jesus affirmed the prohibition against idol food in His messages to the seven churches, once again tying the violation of the rule to the stumbling block. "I have a few things against you," He said, "because you have there some who hold the teaching of Balaam, who kept teaching Balak to put a stumbling block before the sons of Israel, to eat things sacrificed to idols" (Rev. 2:14, NASB).

We must not lose Paul's chief concern in dealing with this lifestyle issue in the early church. What is needed, he says, is self-denying love. Love that denies self for the good of the community is the love that shines from Calvary's cross.

The early church, by settling the issue with a command built on scriptural principle and supported by divine inspiration, thus accomplished three important tasks: 1. It settled a disputed matter and brought unity. Its call for self-denying love supplied a model of action for generations to come. Such actions also illustrated they were not considered legalism or an affront to being saved by grace; rather, they were an outgrowth of the lordship of Christ over His church.

2. It guarded the "little ones"—the new converts—by providing a spiritual nursery. No family can long exist unless it has a safe environment for children. This means the "adults" will abide by certain things they may be at "liberty" to do.

3. It guarded the uniqueness of the whole church and set it aside as distinct and separate from the religions around it.

The Seventh-day Adventist Church today, guided by the Scripture and prophetic gift, calls for its members to be separated from the world through standards of Christian lifestyle. Once again we must help people develop healthy attitudes about these standards and the church authority that gave them. If we applaud Paul's principle, some of the uncertainty, confusion, and debate about these standards might stop. And we might avoid some traps when we apply these standards to our lives.

First, there's the "I've made it" trap. Sincere, truth-loving people easily fall into this one. We need to remind ourselves constantly that we are saved by grace poured out for us on the cross. The umbrella of that grace makes it possible for us to cooperate with Jesus in developing Christlikeness. The church's lifestyle instructions aren't a checklist to show when we have attained Christlikeness. They are, instead, starting points on our pilgrimage.

For instance, let's not consider that Christlikeness in simplicity has been reached when we surrender nonfunctional jewelry. That is only the first step in applying Christ's simplicity to an entire lifestyle. Naturally, the church can't, and shouldn't, tell people how to apply this principle to their car, home, and a host of other things. But as we walk with Jesus and apply this principle, we will rejoice in being able to have more resources to advance the gospel and relieve suffering. By our lives we will send a message that this world is temporary and heaven is our real home.

If Jesus were here today and heard some of these debates, I think He might say something like: "You have heard it said, take off your jewelry. But I say unto you, examine your car, home, and all your possessions in light of the cross." Another example would be the church's position on unclean foods, drugs, alcohol, and tobacco. Does the church or Jesus want us to stop there? Or are we called to grow in healthful living and clear thinking? Lifestyle reforms are basic and foundational. They are not the whole building. We need to look at these standards as beginnings, not finishings; as minimums, not maximums; as a *call* to sanctification, not sanctification.

Then there's the "zealous" trap. People who want to make sure everyone is ready for translation especially face this danger. Our motives may be good, but the methodology is lacking. We find it easy not only to remember every detail of the church standards as listed in the *Church Manual*, but to improve on them.

This isn't surprising, because these "minimums" are unfinished business. The finishing, however, belongs to Jesus. Here

136

again, "knowledge" can get us into trouble. We can become a "stumbling block" by trying to impose an improved list on others. Such an attitude works against the unity of the church just as surely as the one that disregards church standards. The church should provoke an atmosphere for growth—through preaching, teaching, and education. But to insist on imposing additional requirements that the body has not agreed on is to run ahead of Christ.

There's also the "idealistic thinking" trap. This trap is like the "zealous" trap, except the camouflage is different. Here we find sensitive, well-meaning people who are easily embarrassed and who have many questions that sometimes don't get answered. They often question each standard for its consistency, relevancy, and comprehensiveness.

We need to recognize that none of the lifestyle standards are totally consistent. But neither was the prohibition on food offered to idols. To be consistent, the church would have to make rules about everything. Nor will the carnal nature in each of us think such prohibitions are relevant. Certainly the Gentile world must have thought that not eating food offered to idols was crazy. I can hear them now: "What? Can't buy perfectly good food from the market?"

To be totally comprehensive, rules would have to be so specific that volumes would be written. Then we would have maximums, not minimums. Standards don't, can't, and shouldn't speak to all issues. People who fall into this trap often feel the church should just loosen up and let people do what they want to do. "Don't be judgmental" is their theme.

However, the church, in light of Matthew 18, needs to be cautious. "Little ones" are not to be taken lightly. The responsibility is a serious one. God loves His children and does not gladly suffer irresponsible behavior on the part of those who watch over them. Is it not a lack of trust and faith in God when we demand that every question be answered before yielding obedience?

The only way we can avoid these traps is to hear the inspired declaration: "Knowledge puffs up, but love builds up." The restless waves that toss these wonderful lifestyle standards back and forth would be calmed if only our carnal nature would be crucified. The born-again heart, if given a chance, will always embrace self-denying love before arrogant knowledge.

Perhaps we will need a new dose of humility. Perhaps the Western church, with its emphasis on individual freedom, should take a new look at gospel order in light of the New Testament. While some cultures are too quick to accept authority, perhaps the West is too quick to reject it. Just because it's popular to thumb one's nose at any symbol of authority does not mean such a mind-set is part of the born-again spirit. While the Christian is called to stand firm for Jesus, he or she is not called to a rebellious attitude.

We need a new recognition that Jesus is not only Saviour but Lord of our lives. He exercises His lordship not only through the Bible and the gift of prophecy but also through the collective counsel of the church. Adventist leaders and members would do well to reaffirm these calls to holy living. Succumbing to worldly pressures from within and without, most other churches have years ago thrown overboard the treasures we now possess in these standards.

With the coming of Jesus nearer than ever, this is the time to accept these minimums and use them to grow more like Jesus. This is the time to lay aside our "liberties" and deny ourselves for the unity of the body of Christ. This is the time to show our allegiance to each other and provide a safe environment for our "little ones."

Let's say it plainly—this is the time to adhere to church standards and authority whether we think we need them or not. This is the time to be "perfect even as your Father," but to let Him do the perfecting for everyone else. This is the time to practice what we preach—self-sacrificing love. "Knowledge puffs up, but love builds up."

Elder Jay Gallimore is president of the Michigan Conference of Seventh-day Adventists. Born in North Carolina, he graduated from Southern College and Andrews University. He entered the ministry in the Carolina Conference, then went to the Kansas-Nebraska Conference, where he eventually became associate ministerial director. After serving as director for the Northwest Ministries Training Center for the North Pacific Union Conference, he became ministerial director and vice president of the Michigan Conference. He and his wife have two young children.

The Law of God

*T*he great principles of God's law are employed in the Ten Commandments and exemplified in the life of Christ. They express God's love, will, and purposes concerning human conduct and relationships and are binding upon all people in every age. These precepts are the basis of God's covenant with His people and the standard in God's judgment. Through the agency of the Holy Spirit they point out sin and awaken a sense of need for a Saviour. Salvation is all of grace and not of works, but its fruitage is obedience to the Commandments. This obedience develops Christian character and results in a sense of well-being. It is an evidence of our love for the Lord and our concern for our fellow men. The obedience of faith demonstrates the power of Christ to transform lives, and therefore strengthens Christian witness. (Ex. 20:1-17; Ps. 40:7, 8; Matt. 22:36-40; Deut. 28:1-14; Matt. 5:17-20; Heb. 8:8-10; John 16:7-10; Eph. 2:8-10; 1 John 5:3; Rom. 8:3, 4; Ps. 19:7-14.)— Fundamental Beliefs, No. 18.

CHAPTER SEVENTEEN

By John W. Fowler

A Covenant of Love
God's Commandments
Bring Us Good

The *Wall Street Journal* recently took aim at the moral condition of contemporary American society. Referring to the collapse of moral values, the widely respected daily posited the idea that the biblical concept of sin is still valid, particularly in light of the explosion of sexually transmitted diseases in the wake of the sexual revolution of our time. According to the *Journal*, the concept of sin "offered a frame of reference for behavior." "It now appears," said the paper, "that many people could have used a road map." [1]

Referring to the problems of drugs, teenage sex, AIDS, and rape, the editors stated unequivocally that "none of these will go away until people in positions of responsibility come forward and explain, in frankly moral terms, that some of the things people do nowadays are wrong." [2]

The Veil of Humanism

However, few in our morally unrestrained culture have seen the value of the prohibitions found in the Ten Commandments. How strange that a generation that is quick to grasp hold of even the most questionable promises of modern technology, science, and medicine in the pursuit of a better life should fail to see that God's law serves the same purpose. In the face of the most convincing evidence—debilitating disease and the most dreadful forms of death—millions still fail to recognize the validity of the Judeo-Christian value system.

The problem, obscured by a humanistic worldview, is that of

141

the spiritual blindness of the human heart. Consequently, many in today's society have difficulty seeing the practical and helpful wisdom contained in God's law. They regard television tycoon Ted Turner's 10 "initiatives" as a more up-to-date and realistic set of directives for today's complicated world. Proclaiming the prohibitions of the law to the spiritually blind is like cursing the darkness. Only as this blindness is removed can a person see that God's law is a hedge of love about us for our protection.

The light of love can dispel this darkness. This is why Jesus said, "And I, if I be lifted up from the earth, will draw all men unto me" (John 12:32).

The religious leaders of Christ's day focused on the externals of the law. Thus, they failed to recognize the underlying motive of love. Consequently, Jesus spoke of the law in terms of "a new commandment." "A new commandment I give you," He said. "Love one another. As I have loved you, so you must love one another" (John 13:34, NIV). And in Matthew 22:37-40 He interpreted the Ten Commandments in the context of love to God and love for others.

Thus, Christ set forth the law, not in the context of strict and arbitrary demands, but in the atmosphere of loving, redemptive relationships. Going far beyond the prohibitive "don'ts" of the Ten Commandments, Jesus presented the law as beatitudes, blessings. When questioned as to which commandment was the greatest, He used no "Thou shalt not's." Rather, He said, "Love the Lord your God with all your heart. . . . Love your neighbor as yourself. There is no commandment greater than these" (Mark 12:30, 31, NIV).

Why is it so important to see that the law speaks of love? Because "only by love is love awakened." [3] And once love is awakened, it will never intentionally do anything wrong or hurtful. Love always builds up and makes stronger; it never tears down or destroys. This is why Paul says that "love is the fulfilling of the law" (Rom. 13:10).

It is in this context that the law provides the road map that could have protected this generation from the death and destruction following in the wake of the moral and sexual revolution of the past few decades. This law of love is "a lamp to my feet and a light for my path" (Ps. 119:105, NIV), guiding us in the way that leads to meaningful and purposeful living. God reminds us that our peace and happiness grow out of obedience to the law. "If only you had paid attention to my commands, your peace would have been like a river, your righteousness like the waves of the sea" (Isa. 48:18, NIV).

Seventh-day Adventists are big on the law. And rightly so. It is no accident that our name highlights the importance of the law. The remnant church of Revelation is identified by the fact that it honors and upholds the law. However, any honest observer has to ask: Do we recognize that Christ defined the law in the context of loving, redemptive relationships? And do we love as Christ loved? We must admit that we have often failed miserably.

Love to God

The first table of the law focuses on a loving relationship with God. Christ is our standard. In His love to the Father, He demonstrated those steadfast qualities described by the law. He spent quality time alone with the Father in secret prayer and communion. "Rising up a great while before day, he went out, and departed into a solitary place, and there prayed" (Mark 1:35). "He withdrew himself into the wilderness, and prayed" (Luke 5:16). "And it came to pass in those days, that he went out into a mountain to pray, and continued all night in prayer to God" (Luke 6:12).

Christ's love for His Father also kept Him in conscious awareness of the Father's presence. He found in this intimate relationship His greatest satisfaction and joy, His deepest peace and strength. Ellen G. White points out that "His hours of happiness were found when alone with nature and God." [4] If we allow the law of love to guide us, we, with the psalmist, can know this joy. "You have made known to me the path of life; you will fill me with joy in your presence, with eternal pleasures at your right hand" (Ps. 16:11, NIV).

Rightly understood, the law calls us into this relationship with God, bringing meaning and purpose to our lives. And this love relationship with God, nurtured by the law, brings to us a sense of identity, a realization of who we are. We are led to a heightened

143

consciousness of being, to a sense of self-worth, security, and permanence.

Because of a misunderstanding of the law of God, millions today either have never known or have lost this relationship with God. Consequently, they are disjointed and disconnected.

Their hearts are empty, aching for something the world can never fill. They wander in the wilderness of this scientific age, prodigals estranged from their heavenly Father, not aware that joy and peace can be found only as they return to their heavenly Father's house. A proper understanding of the law of love opens the door to this relationship with the great God who created us for His own fellowship. And once we have this abiding relationship with Christ, we will see that the law's external prohibitions serve only to enhance this joyful reality.

Love for Another

The second table of the law guides us in our relationship with one another. Again Christ's love for others demonstrates the standard of heaven itself. Christ was always patient and kind, always tender and compassionate. "He did not censure human weakness." [5] In fact, He never took the first step in severing His relationship with any individual.

The cross reveals that Jesus chose to allow His accusers and murderers to take His life rather than break His relationship with them.

The law promises this quality of love in our relationships with one another. It is the same quality revealed in a mother's love that will follow a son or daughter into the gutter, to prison, or to the electric chair. God's great heart of love goes out to those most hopelessly entangled in sin.

As we come into possession of this love, we will overlook one another's faults and weaknesses. We will forgive one another in spite of shortcomings. Genuine love will enable even those who disagree theologically to love one another.

Abraham Lincoln demonstrated such love in his relations with Edwin M. Stanton, who as U.S. secretary of war often criticized and opposed the president. Once when the president sent orders to

Stanton on details of troop operations in the war, Stanton called Lincoln a fool.

Back at the White House the messenger told Lincoln what had happened. "Did Stanton say I was a fool?" asked the president. "He did, sir," replied the messenger, "and repeated it."

Lincoln paused a moment, then replied, "If Stanton said I was a fool, then I must be one. For he is nearly always right. I will step over and see him." [6]

Lincoln and Stanton eventually developed a cordial and trusting relationship. As Lincoln lay on his deathbed, it was Stanton who, fighting back tears, said, "Now he belongs to the ages." [7]

How much we need such love today!

"He drew a circle that shut me out—
Heretic, rebel, a thing to flout.
But love and I had the wit to win,
We drew a circle that took him in!" [8]

Very often we do just the opposite. Consider a couple going through divorce. Often, rather than drawing the couple close to us, we distance ourselves from them. If the divorcing couple does not have biblical grounds, the *Church Manual* suggests that we disfellowship them.

I hope you will not misunderstand me in this. I believe we must uphold the sanctity of marriage and underscore the evils of divorce. Yet do we really want to break our fellowship with those going through a divorce at a time when they need us the most? I believe we should uphold the church's policy. But do we want to withhold our love and support from those suffering from the death of the most intimate and meaningful human relationship known to us?

Love demands that we find a way to make a strong statement regarding Christian morality, while at the same time keeping those tempted and overcome within our circle of love. Christ revealed this balance in His ministry.

Love for the World

Christ's statement in John 13:34 that we are to love one another encircles the whole human family. The law given at Sinai is equally applicable to all people, calling us into a responsible relationship to those who do not know Christ.

Again, Christ's work in the world is the standard. He came to live in our world, to share our circumstances, to carry our burdens, to suffer with and for us, to redeem and restore us to Himself. In the same way, the Christian is to go into the world to make it a better place to live, to help resolve its problems. We are to care for the needy and destitute, to feed the hungry, and clothe the naked. We are to bring healing to the diseased and hope to the dying. We are to address problems of justice, human rights, racial prejudice, religious freedom, and the environment.

But while working in these important areas, we must keep in mind that our transcendent goal is to seek out people in their lostness and restore them to a meaningful relationship with their Creator. If we wish to be approved at the last, then we must remember that no intellectual superiority, or eloquence in preaching, or absorption in business, or timidity can excuse us for not making an honest, sincere, prayerful effort to win others to Christ by means of the personal touch.

Putting It All Together

How are we then to bring this love into all our relationships? Christ is the answer. He alone can give us this divine love.

By beholding Christ we are changed. "But we all, with unveiled face, beholding as in a mirror the glory of the Lord, are being transformed into the same image from glory to glory, just as by the Spirit of the Lord" (2 Cor. 3:18, NKJV).

This divine love, revealed by the law and seen in the life of Christ, graphically underscores our need. It draws us to Christ, who alone can engender it. We are to behold Christ's condescension in becoming human, His life of self-denying service, His suffering and death on the cross, His resurrection and soon return. But especially His cross. In this work of redemption He was fulfilling the law of love and life that guarantees the security and happiness of the universe.

Only as we surrender our lives to Christ can God's Spirit write this law in our hearts, only then can we practice it in the church and demonstrate it in the world.

"Were the whole realm of nature mine,
That were a tribute far too small;
Love so amazing, so divine,
Demands my life, my soul, my all." [9]

---

[1] Daniel Henniger, "The Joy of What?" *The Wall Street Journal,* Jan. 8, 1992.

[2] *Ibid.*

[3] *The Desire of Ages,* p. 22.

[4] *Ibid.,* p. 90.

[5] *Steps to Christ,* p. 12.

[6] Carl Sandburg, *Abraham Lincoln: The Prairie Years and the War Years* (New York: Dell Pub. Co., Inc., 1967), vol. 2, p. 264.

[7] Stephen B. Oates, *With Malice Toward None* (New York: New American Library, 1977), p. 471.

[8] Edwin Markham, "Outwitted."

[9] Isaac Watts, in *The Seventh-day Adventist Hymnal,* No. 155.

John Wesley Fowler is conference secretary of the Kentucky-Tennessee Conference. A graduate of Southern College and Andrews University, he has served as pastor, evangelist, ministerial secretary on the conference and union level, and conference president. He is working on a doctorate in preaching. His hobbies include hiking, camping, tennis, and collecting old books.

The Holy Spirit

God the eternal Spirit was active with the Father and the Son in Creation, incarnation, and redemption. He inspired the writers of Scripture. He filled Christ's life with power. He draws and convicts human beings; and those who respond He renews and transforms into the image of God. Sent by the Father and the Son to be always with His children, He extends spiritual gifts to the church, empowers it to bear witness to Christ, and in harmony with the Scriptures leads it into all truth. (Gen. 1:1, 2; Luke 1:35; 4:18; Acts 10:38; 2 Peter 1:21; 2 Cor. 3:18; Eph. 4:11, 12; Acts 1:8; John 14:16-18, 26; 15:26, 27; 16:7-13.)—Fundamental Beliefs, No. 5.

CHAPTER EIGHTEEN

By *Arnold V. Wallenkampf*

The Holy Spirit
God's Power to Transform and Empower

Wh
hen you think of the Holy Spirit, do your thoughts center primarily on His *power* or on His *guidance?*

There is no question about His power. Jesus said, "All power [authority] is given unto me in heaven and in earth" (Matt. 28:18, KJV).* The promised power is twofold: first, power for personal moral growth toward transformation of character into Christ's likeness (see Rom. 12:2; 2 Cor. 3:18). Then power is assured God's workers to make them effective in their service for Him.

Today the Holy Spirit, Christ's representative on earth, is holding this authority and power in hand. Not hoarding it, but holding it for you and me, eager to make it available to any member of God's family on earth who follows God's will and seeks to do God's work.

Before Jesus left His disciples He gave them this promise: "You shall receive power when the Holy Spirit has come upon you; and you shall be my witnesses" (Acts 1:8). But the promise of power to the disciples would be fulfilled only after they had been "baptized with the Holy Spirit" (verse 5).

The promised baptism of the Holy Spirit was not the disciples' first acquaintance with Him. They had already received "the Holy Spirit" (John 20:22), but not in fullness.

From Creation's morning it was God's plan that every intelligent, free-willed being should be indwelt by the Spirit. In sin-free Eden God placed the Spirit in Adam and Eve. "From eternal ages it was God's purpose that every created being, from the bright and holy seraph to man, should be a temple for the indwelling of the

149

Creator. Because of sin, humanity ceased to be a temple for God." [1]
The Holy Spirit within Adam and Eve was a sign that they
belonged to God and recognized God's lordship.

Early ranchers in the western part of the United States used to
raise their cattle on open range. In this way cattle belonging to one
herd mixed with those from other herds. For identification purposes, however, each rancher was required by law to put a brand
on each animal.

The brand was an owner's special mark burned into the
animal's forehead and side. Wherever the animal roamed, even
among thousands of look-alikes, it could easily be identified with
its owner.

God's Mark on Us

As ranchers brand their cattle, so God puts His spiritual brand
on every sinner who turns to Him in repentance. God's sign of
ownership is the gift of the Holy Spirit. This is in keeping with
Peter's promise to the contrite crowd who cried to him on the day
of Pentecost, "Brethren, what shall we do?" His reply was "Repent,
and be baptized . . . ; and you shall receive the gift of the Holy
Spirit" (Acts 2:37, 38).

The gift of the Spirit, given at conversion, is God's universal
seal given to everyone who accepts His lordship. Through the new
birth (see John 3:3-7) God purposes that mankind shall again
become indwelt by the Holy Spirit. Paul testified to that when he
wrote to the Corinthian believers, "You are God's temple and . . .
God's Spirit dwells in you" (1 Cor. 3:16; cf. 6:19). "Any one who
does not have the Spirit of Christ does not belong to him" (Rom.
8:9).

The Holy Spirit is God's "seal of ownership on us" and "a
deposit guaranteeing what is to come" (2 Cor. 1:22, NIV; cf. Eph.
1:13; 4:30). The Holy Spirit in the believer's heart is God's
downpayment and assurance that every person who chooses to
remain in God will be fitted for heavenly society.

The seal of the Holy Spirit is not to be confused with the
universal grace of God that strives with every person, even before
conversion.

In addition to God's universal agelong seal, God also has an eschatological seal, spoken of in Revelation 7 and comparable to that in Ezekiel 9. This seal guarantees protection amid impending destruction. This eschatological seal all God's faithful followers will receive in the very end-time before the falling of the plagues of Revelation 15 and 16. Both this end-time seal of God and its opposite, the mark of the beast, are still in the future.

The seal of God's Holy Spirit should, furthermore, be distinguished from the Spirit baptism Jesus promised His disciples (see Acts 1:5). When this promise was fulfilled on the day of Pentecost, Luke did not speak of it as a baptism or a sealing, but as being "filled with the Holy Spirit" (Acts 2:4).

After this the believers in the apostolic church were repeatedly filled with the Spirit (see Acts 4:8, 31; 6:3, 5; 7:55; 9:17; 13:9, 52; 19:6; cf. 6:5; 11:24). Paul admonished the Ephesian believers who had already been sealed with the Spirit (see Eph. 1:13; 4:30): "Do not get drunk with wine, for that is debauchery; but be filled with the Spirit" (Eph. 5:18).

The word "baptism" and its corresponding verb come from a word meaning immersion. The believers ideally were to be immersed in the Spirit, covered by the Spirit, surrounded by the Spirit, and filled with the Spirit—as the drunkard is filled with liquor. In other words, they were to be completely under the Spirit's control, as a drunkard is under the control of his inebriation. Being baptized with the Spirit and being filled with the Spirit seem to denote the same experience.

A Divine Person

Jesus' chief discourse on the coming of the Holy Spirit is found in John 14-16. By studying these chapters it becomes clear that the Holy Spirit is a person and part of Deity—together with God the Father and God the Son.[2]

During His time with the disciples Jesus had been their counselor. After His departure the Holy Spirit was to take His place as their counselor, teacher, and guide. The Spirit would remind them of Christ's teachings, guide them into all truth, and reveal to them what was yet to come. Included in this guidance was conviction of sin, of righteousness, and of judgment.

Jesus assured His disciples, distraught at His announcement

that He was about to depart, that He would not leave them orphans. Rather, He would ask the Father to give them "another Counselor"—one like Himself—who would be with them forever. Jesus called this Representative the *Paraclete*.

There is no word in the English language fully adequate to express the meaning of "Paraclete." The Holy Spirit is more than "Comforter," more than "Counselor" (as the word "paraclete" is translated in the King James and the Revised Standard versions, respectively). The Spirit is also our advocate (as paraclete is translated in 1 John 2:1) and helper (as other Bible translations have it). The Holy Spirit is given to every child of God and is a helper adequate for any situation and need.

To me, the Paraclete is heaven's ambassador plenipotentiary, invested with all of heaven's authority, wisdom, wealth, and power; cradled in God's love and our Saviour's grace. In the promise of the Holy Spirit, Jesus gave His followers, as it were, a blank check signed in His blood—a blank check payable with all the resources of heaven!

To be sealed with the Spirit does not mean that the recipient is instantly changed. Rather, it means that the Spirit has moved into the life of the willing convert, there to begin the work of change from rebellion to glad-hearted obedience.

It is worth noting that Jesus, in His parable in Matthew 12:43-45, likened the soul temple to a house. The parable emphasizes that a person's soul temple must not, and cannot, remain vacant. Someone or something must needs occupy it. At conversion the Holy Spirit enters the sinner's heart, not as a houseguest, but ideally to be the permanent tenant and a constant mentor.

From the foyer of the soul temple, so to speak, the Spirit moves into the living room, into the kitchen, the family room, the bedroom. The Spirit examines the picture on the wall, the food in the refrigerator, the programs we enjoy in the family room, our activities in the bedroom. And in every area of our lives He brings about change and transformation.

Under the guidance of the Spirit the new convert learns that the true Christian is a steward under God of his body, time, and possessions. The Spirit is a guide for both his desires and plans. He is the regenerating agent who personalizes and makes individually effective for all the salvation wrought by the death of Christ on the cross.

We should remember, however, that not all Christians are at the same growth level. Therefore, not all followers of Christ are alike, although their commitment to Him may be equally whole-hearted. The principle of growth, applicable to plants and enunci-ated by Jesus, applies also to Christians (see Mark 4:28).

Gradually experiencing change in both thinking and lifestyle, we will come to reflect God's will more and more fully. Ultimately, we will be fully under the control of the Holy Spirit and "be filled with all the fulness of God" (Eph. 3:19). This was Paul's hope for every believer. Thus, we become a more effective witness.

Daniel and the three Hebrew youth serve as examples of people who were not only sealed with the Spirit but apparently also baptized and filled with the Spirit, trusting God fully. That's why they were ready to die rather than depart from God's known will for them (see Dan. 3 and 6).

No Guarantee

But as neither engagement nor the wedding ceremony can guarantee the durability of marriage, just so neither the seal of God nor the fullness of the Spirit can guarantee a person's eternal salvation. After pledging our allegiance to God, we will, as in a marriage, possess freedom of choice. We can still change our minds. Early in his life King Saul had the Spirit of God come mightily upon him (see 1 Sam. 10:10; 11:6). But after persistently going against the will of God, the Holy Spirit was ultimately withdrawn from him (see 1 Sam. 16:14). Thus Saul, who had once been mighty through the Spirit, "died for his unfaithfulness" (1 Chron. 10:13). We should therefore remember that the posses-sion of the Holy Spirit does not free the recipient from either temptation or trial. Spirit-endued Saul was tempted, and he failed.

I can recall several occasions when I knew God's will but did not like it. But then I prayed, "God, I cannot change my attitude or heart, but You can do it. For You have said, 'A new heart I will give you, and a new spirit I will put within you; and I will take out of your flesh the heart of stone and give you a heart of flesh. And I will put my spirit within you' [Eze. 36:26, 27]. Please, God, fulfill that promise to me so that I may want to follow Your will."

This promise God has fulfilled for me several times. And He will do it for all of us, provided we are willing. "You are not able, of yourself, to bring your purposes and desires and inclinations into submission to the will of God; but if you are 'willing to be made willing,' God will accomplish the work for you, even 'casting down imaginations, and every high thing that exalteth itself against the knowledge of God, and bringing into captivity every thought to the obedience of Christ' (2 Cor. 10:5)." [3]

We can have the assurance that after a person accepts Jesus as his or her Saviour, God will never *initiate* a divorce. God vows that "him who comes to me I will not cast out" (John 6:37). And Jesus assures us: "My Father, who has given [you] to me, is greater than all, and no one is able to snatch [you] out of my Father's hand" (John 10:20).

Our eternal salvation rests neither on being sealed nor on being baptized and filled with the Spirit. Rather, it is anchored in our remaining in Christ. Jesus Himself says, "He who endures to the end will be saved" (Matt. 24:13).

After the Ascension the disciples and their fellow believers gathered in the upper room desiring to know and follow God's will and guidance. In this they "were all with one accord" (Acts 2:1, KJV). No longer were they interested in personal position and power, although that had been everyone's concern when they had met for the Last Supper. In the upper room they were all emptied of self.

As a result, they were baptized and filled with the Spirit, becoming Spirit-directed people. In their evangelizing ministry the apostolic believers were but executing God's revealed will. They gladly acted in conformity with the Spirit's biddings.

The apostolic believers lived at the beginning of the gospel era. Spirit-filled and Spirit-directed, their gospel proclamation was edged with the power of the Holy Spirit. As a result, they "turned the world upside down" (Acts 17:6), evangelizing the then-known world (see Col. 1:6, 23).

We the members of the remnant church are living at the very end of the gospel dispensation, standing on the very brink of eternity, when God—not we—"will finish the work, and cut it short in righteousness" (Rom. 9:28, KJV).

But God is yearning for us to join Him in finishing His work. We too may become effective instruments in His hand as we, like the apostolic believers, choose to be Spirit-filled and Spirit-directed. As God baptized and filled them with His Spirit, so He is eager to fill us also with His Spirit. He is even more eager to do it than are parents to give good gifts to their children (see Luke 11:13). With this awareness comes the lavish reminder that "if all were willing, all would be filled with the Spirit." [4]

Lord, make us willing!

---

* Unless otherwise noted, Bible texts in this chapter are from the Revised Standard Version.

---

[1] *The Desire of Ages,* p. 161.

[2] For scriptural support for the personhood and deity of the Holy Spirit, see the author's book *New by the Spirit* (Mountain View, Calif.: Pacific Press Pub. Assn., 1978), chapters 1, 2.

[3] *Thoughts From the Mount of Blessing,* p. 142.

[4] *The Acts of the Apostles,* p. 50.

Born in Sweden, Arnold V. Wallenkampf has had a long and varied denominational career. He has been a pastor and a religion teacher on the academy, college, and graduate levels. Fluent in seven languages, he has authored many books and Sabbath school lesson quarterlies. Until his retirement he was associate director of the Biblical Research Institute at the General Conference. The Wallenkampfs are retired in Virginia, where they are active in their local church.

# *The Second Coming*

*T*he second coming of Christ is the blessed hope of the church, the grand climax of the gospel. The Saviour's coming will be literal, personal, visible, and worldwide. When He returns, the righteous dead will be resurrected, and together with the righteous living will be glorified and taken to heaven, but the unrighteous will die. The almost complete fulfillment of most lines of prophecy, together with the present condition of the world, indicates that Christ's coming is imminent. The time of that event has not been revealed, and we are therefore exhorted to be ready at all times. *(Titus 2:13; Heb. 9:28; John 14:1-3; Acts 1:9-11; Matt. 24:14; Rev. 1:7; Matt. 26:43, 44; 1 Thess. 4:13-18; 1 Cor. 15:51-54; 2 Thess. 1:7-10; 2:8; Rev. 14:14-20; 19:11-21; Matt. 24; Mark 13; Luke 21; 2 Tim. 3:1-5; 1 Thess. 5:1-6.)*—Fundamental Beliefs, *No.* 24.

CHAPTER NINETEEN

By Marvin Moore

The Second Coming
Our Planet's Only Hope

One day a father told his 5-year-old son that he would be going on a long trip. "But I will return," he said.

"How will I know when you're coming back?" the little boy asked.

The father thought a moment, and then said, "When you see leaves all over the backyard, you can know that I will be coming soon."

Each day after his father left, the little boy ran outside and checked the ground for leaves. As autumn approached, the trees turned various shades of red and yellow, and one night a strong wind blew. The next morning the little boy made his usual trip outside, and this time he found the yard covered with leaves. "Daddy's coming home!" he yelled as he ran around kicking up the leaves. "Daddy's coming home!"

The Bible tells a similar story. It happened during the Last Supper. Jesus knew that His time with the disciples was drawing to a close. Soon He would die on a cross, and a few days after that He would take a "long trip" to heaven.

"My children," He said, "I will be with you only a little longer. . . . Where I am going, you cannot come" (John 13:33).*

The disciples felt deeply distressed. "Where are you going?" Peter asked. "Why can't [we] follow you?" (verses 36, 37).

Jesus replied with those well-known words: "Do not let your hearts be troubled. . . . If I go . . . I will come again" (John 14:1-3).

The Second Coming is the blessed hope of Christians. To fully understand it, we have to know something of God's original plan

157

for our world and the conflict between good and evil that has been raging here for more than 6,000 years.

God's Original Plan

God intended that Adam and Eve and all their descendants should be supremely happy. Had His plan been carried out, the word *grief* would never have made it into the dictionary. Not one tear would ever have been spilled onto a grave. Not one child would ever have been struck down by a car. Not one mother would ever have been torn from her children by a terminal disease.

These tragedies have happened because an enemy invaded Adam and Eve's happy home and they yielded to his temptation. Immediately their hearts were transformed, and a cruel, sinful nature has distorted the life of every human being from that day to this. The creation itself—the world of nature—"has been groaning as in the pains of childbirth" (Rom. 8:22).

Is there no hope? Is there no escape from this terrible fate? Yes, there is! God promised Eve that Jesus, her offspring, would crush Satan's head (see Gen. 3:15). Satan would be destroyed, and all of Jesus' faithful followers would be restored to the perfect world He originally planned for them.

That's why the second coming of Jesus is so important. It's the time when God will fulfill His promise to Eve. He will remove His people from the broken world they've been in for more than 6,000 years and reinstate them in that perfect home.

Is it any wonder that God's people from the time of Adam and Eve to the present have looked so anxiously for the second coming of Jesus? Enoch said, "See, the Lord is coming with thousands upon thousands of his holy ones" (Jude 14). Abraham looked forward to a city "with foundations, whose architect and builder is God" (Heb. 11:10).

Isaiah prophesied of "new heavens and [a] new earth," where "from one Sabbath to another, all mankind will come and bow down" before God (Isa. 66:22, 23).

John said, "Even so, come, Lord Jesus" (Rev. 22:20, KJV), and God's faithful people throughout Christian history have said, "How long, O Lord"—how much longer do we have to wait for Your appearing? (Rev. 6:10, KJV).

Seventh-day Adventists, along with many other Christians, believe that we live very near the time when this "blessed hope" will be fulfilled. This gives us great joy—to know that soon the sorrow we experience in this life will be over.

Earth's Final War

However, the second coming of Jesus will be more than the time when God takes His people to heaven. It will also be the time when our world will be torn from Satan's grasp and given to its rightful Ruler, Jesus Christ.

Thousands of years ago Satan established a beachhead on this earth from which he expected to launch his attack against God throughout the universe. Naturally, he doesn't want his dominion over the world taken away, and he will do everything in his power to keep that from happening.

Revelation, especially the last half, gives a detailed description of Satan's supreme effort to interfere with Christ's second coming. God's people who live on earth at that time will be deeply involved in this conflict. "The dragon was enraged at the woman and went off to make war against the rest of her offspring—those who obey God's commandments and hold to the testimony of Jesus" (Rev. 12:17).

There was war in heaven when rebellion first broke out. At that time it was Michael and His angels against Satan and his angels. However, in earth's final war, just before Jesus comes, it will be Christ and His loyal followers on earth against Satan and his human followers.

Satan and his allies will take control of the entire world, and they will use their superior position to attack God's people: "He [the first beast of Revelation 13] was given authority over every tribe, people, language and nation," and "he was given power to make war against the saints and to conquer them" (Rev. 13:7).

However, earth's wicked inhabitants will do far more than attack God's people. *Puny human beings will actually fight against the God of the universe!* Revelation 17:14 says that the 10 kings of Revelation 17 will "make war against the Lamb." In vision John saw "the beast and the kings of the earth and their armies

159

gathered together to make war against the rider on the horse and his army" (Rev. 19:19).

I believe that the world's political and military leaders will join with Satan in a desperate attempt to prevent Jesus from coming to this world. Two factors make this realistic.

First are the powerful weapons of mass destruction that earth's military leaders have at their disposal today. They may very well flatter themselves that they can launch their missiles into space and block Christ and His angels—an "alien race"—from invading the world.

Second are the miracle-working demons that earth's military leaders will have on their side. These demons can call fire down from heaven and perform many other signs and wonders. In league with these powerful beings, the world's generals will think they can do anything (see Rev. 16:13, 14).

Armageddon

This will be the battle of Armageddon, which the world has puzzled over ever since John wrote the Revelation. The battle of Armageddon is closely associated with the second coming of Christ. In fact, it *is* the second coming of Christ.

Revelation 19:11-16 pictures Christ at His second coming as an army general riding from heaven on a white horse, followed by soldiers who are also riding white horses. And verses 17-21 describe the combined military forces of the world that He will engage in battle. Revelation 19 describes Christ's second coming as a war between heaven's armies and the armies of earth. And the army of heaven will win (verses 20, 21).

Jesus will also use physical weapons in His counterattack. His weapons will be the forces of nature: earthquakes, hailstones, thunder and lightning, mountains collapsing and islands disappearing into the sea. The description is awesome beyond comprehension. Think of what the world would have looked like had the United States and the Soviet Union unleashed their atomic warheads against each other during the height of the cold war. Why should the world fare any better when the God of the universe engages it in battle? No wonder Jeremiah describes the aftermath of this war as a dark, desolate earth, devoid of human life, its fields

160

a desert and its towns in ruins (see Jer. 4:23-26).

Yet you and I need not be afraid as we anticipate this war, for He will cover us with His feathers, and under His wings we will find refuge. "A thousand may fall at your side, ten thousand at your right hand," the psalmist says, but it will not come near us. No harm will come upon us because He will command His angels to guard us in all our ways (Ps. 91:4-11).

Here's how Ellen White describes God's people during this time: "I saw the leading men of the earth consulting together. . . . I saw a writing . . . giving orders that unless the saints should yield their peculiar faith, . . . the people were at liberty after a certain time to put them to death. *But in this hour of trial the saints were calm and composed, trusting in God and leaning upon His promise that a way of escape would be made for them*" (*Early Writings*, pp. 282, 283; emphasis supplied).

Not a Time for Weaklings

I don't mean that earth's final conflict will be like a Sunday afternoon picnic. This will not be a time for spiritual weaklings. Only those who have fortified their minds with the truths of God's Word will be able to escape the deceptions of the last days, and only those who have fortified their spirits with the faith of God's Word will escape the intense pressures of the last days.

But for God's elect this will be both a trying time and a time of great joy. Jesus said that when the multitudes of the world are terrified at the signs of Christ's return, you and I will rejoice and lift up our heads, because we will see that our redemption is drawing near (see Luke 21:25-28).

Why will we be able to do this *then?* Because we are learning to trust Him *now*. When Jesus responded to the disciples' question about the signs of His coming, He spent far more time telling them how to be prepared than He did telling them what the world's final events would actually be like or how they would know when they are near.

And the bottom line of Jesus' advice was this: We must have the oil—a relationship with Him through the Holy Spirit. We must use our talents in His work. And through His transforming grace

AP-6

we must keep our hearts filled with love for other people (see Matt. 25).

It will be too late to obtain that relationship with Jesus when the storm breaks. We must be cultivating that relationship now. We do that through Bible study, prayer, fellowship, and other spiritual disciplines that God has provided. We do it by trusting God in the little difficulties that come our way today. We do it by learning not to complain when life doesn't go just the way we think it should.

I look forward to the second coming of Jesus with great joy. It will be the most traumatic event in all of earth's history, but to you and me that trauma will simply be the birth pangs by which we are ushered into our eternal home. During that terrible time, the second coming of Jesus will be the blessed hope of God's people as never before.

That's why, when I see the multiplying signs of His coming, I can "run around the backyard," kicking up the leaves and exclaiming, "Daddy's coming to take me home! Daddy's coming to take me home!"

---

*Unless otherwise noted, Bible texts in this chapter are from the New International Version.

The son of missionary parents, Marvin Moore was born in Lima, Peru, and lived in Argentina and Cuba before coming to the United States to complete his secondary and college education. After earning degrees from Union College and Andrews University, he pastored in California and Texas. During the 1970s he was self-employed as a free-lance writer. In 1985 he became associate book editor at Pacific Press Publishing Association, and is currently acquisitions editor there. He is also working on a Doctor of Ministry degree through Andrews University.

The Remnant and Its Mission

*T*he universal church is composed of all who truly believe in Christ, but in the last days, a time of widespread apostasy, a remnant has been called out to keep the commandments of God and the faith of Jesus. This remnant announces the arrival of the judgment hour, proclaims salvation through Christ, and heralds the approach of His second advent. This proclamation is symbolized by the three angels of Revelation 14; it coincides with the work of judgment in heaven and results in a work of repentance and reform on earth. Every believer is called to have a personal part in this worldwide witness. (Rev. 12:17; 14:6-12; 18:1-4; 2 Cor. 5:10; Jude 3, 14; 1 Peter 1:16-19; 2 Peter 3:10-14; Rev. 21:1-14.)— Fundamental Beliefs, *No. 12.*

CHAPTER TWENTY
By John Dybdahl

Our Mission
We Are Sent to People

Mission involves sending. Missionaries (ones sent) go with the message of Jesus across a border. The real border they cross is the one between faith and unbelief, between the church and the world.

Mission offers life. Life abundant comes to unbelievers when they follow Jesus. Life for the church comes from faithfulness to its mission. Where there is no mission, the church perishes. Death culminates a painful, often lingering period of weakness and sickness. The church needs mission to remain alive and well.

I never expected to see this death process begin in the Hmong village of Huey Hai, Thailand. When I first visited this village in the early 1970s, a few members of a prominent family had just become Adventists. Excitement about the freedom and joy Jesus brought them pervaded their lives. They rejoiced because the old way of spirit worship based on fear no longer bound them. Eagerly they shared the new message with fellow villagers, and within a few years most of the village became Christian. They built a church and started a school.

Fifteen years later young people from the village told me a sad story. Many older members no longer attended church. Members quarreled with each other, and many disliked the pastor. The church had turned inward and was feeding on itself. Having completed its mission to win the village, it had *failed* to catch a vision for mission beyond the village limits, and had nothing on which to use its energy except internal wrangling.

Huey Hai is the story of every individual, local church, confer-

165

ence, mission, union, division, or denomination that loses its mission. The principle is a universal one—lose your mission, and you lose your spiritual life!

Mission and the Bible

The Bible speaks clearly of the general task of mission. According to Matthew, Jesus' final command to His disciples was to "Go therefore and make disciples of all nations" (Matt. 28:19).* Mark quotes Jesus in similar words: "Go into all the world and preach the gospel to the whole creation" (Mark 16:15). And Jesus said, "You shall be my witnesses in Jerusalem and in all Judea and Samaria, and to the end of the earth" (Acts 1:8). These passages are vital, for they make several important points about mission clear.

First, Jesus is behind the mission. According to the New Testament the source of mission is our Saviour and Lord, not some human being or church tradition. Missionaries are sent by Jesus. The call does not come from some church leader or organization.

Second, the mission is based on Jesus' final words and express command. Final words are crucial and important words—words that are meant to be remembered and followed. These words are a *command*—not just a wish. This is the Great Commission, not just a great suggestion or one great option for a church that claims to follow Jesus.

Third, the mission is a universal one. The message is to reach the whole world and every creature. No place or person can be left out. All need Jesus.

Fourth, as made clear from other passages, this mission lasts until "the end" (Matt. 24:14), or "the close of the age" (Matt. 28:20). The mission ends only when time as we know it ends.

In this mission, what is the message? The message has to do with Jesus. The messengers are to "make disciples" (Matt. 28:19) for Jesus. They are to "preach the gospel," for they are "my [i.e., Jesus'] witnesses" (Mark 16:15; Acts 1:8). The message is a proclamation of the gospel or good news about Jesus and a call for people to follow *this* Jesus as disciples.

These great truths about mission are so crucial that they make or break the church. As mission goes, so goes the church. The church must possess a sense of mission, articulate and understand that mission, and efficiently excuse that mission if it plans to obey the Lord.

Mission and Church History

Many church historians teach that theology and the development of doctrine constitute the great shapers and moving forces behind Christian history. Adventists have always taken belief seriously, but we need to realize mission is as basic a force as doctrine.

What if Paul and others had not gone as missionaries to Europe—especially Greece and Rome, among other places?

What if Pope Gregory X in A.D. 1271 had responded powerfully to Kublai Khan's call for missionaries to China? What if instead of sending a pitiful two-monk missionary force that turned back in Armenia, the pope had launched a massive missionary effort?[1]

What if Adventists had not clearly developed the vision for a worldwide mission? We would be a small, mainly North American denomination like the Advent Christian Church. Even now the non-North American nature of our church members is mightily affecting our church policy, structure, practice, and even doctrine. Mission is the great shaper of our town today.

Keeping Mission Alive

As we look to the future, what must we understand and believe if we want to keep mission alive and vibrant in our lives and in our church? I suggest four major points:

First, *we must have a vision for the unreached peoples and areas of our world*. Both home and foreign mission are crucial. We must work in our town culturally and cross-culturally as well. In tough economic times, pressure always exists to keep money for local needs. We must remember the divine principle—that helping those far away has a beneficial effect on the work at home.

"To show a liberal, self-denying spirit for the success of foreign missions is a sure way to advance home missionary work; for the prosperity of the home work depends largely, under God, upon the reflex influence of the evangelical work done in countries afar off." [2]

167

Many do not realize how big the remaining task is. Although exact figures vary, most agree that more than 2 billion people in the world will be able to learn the gospel only if someone crosses culture to come to them. That is about 40 percent of the world's population.[3]

Our church's Global Mission program has studied and identified these unreached peoples. We should *all* be involved in reaching out to them.

Second, *we must live close to the sin, hurts, and lost state of the world so we can be moved by the need.* There are too many Seventh-day Adventist ghettos and too many second-, third-, and fourth-generation Adventists who have forgotten or not seen and experienced the world's pain.

Repeatedly I have seen college students changed by going as student missionaries or by taking part in mission trips. Going on mission trips elicits deeper commitment to that mission. If we want people to help heal a sick world, we must seek ways to help them see, taste, hear, and feel its sickness.

Third, *we must clearly state our message to the other world religions and to secular people.* Many Adventists have spent most of their time articulating their beliefs in the context of *other Christians.* When we meet Muslims, Buddhists, Hindus, and secularists, we are ill-equipped. We can't teach the Sabbath if the listener doesn't accept Jesus or the Bible. We must learn anew the beauty of the basics of Christianity—the most basic of basics is, of course, Jesus. My encounter with Buddhists during the early years of my ministry forced me back to Jesus, and I've never been the same since.

Strange as it may seem, Adventists have more in common with major non-Christian religions than other major Christian denominations do. When we meet Jews, we share a common day of worship, a keen interest in the Old Testament, and in the Bible's food laws. Muslims share our disdain for pork and alcohol and appreciate our stand against worldly amusements. Millions of middle- and high-caste Hindus are vegetarians. So also are numerous Buddhists. And Hindus and Buddhists are sympathetic to our stand on noncombatancy.

The Adventist emphasis on the whole person is generally

appreciated by all these religions. Their beliefs tend to embrace more of their lives than does the religion of typical Western Christians, and they like our wholistic teaching.

Another huge segment of our world is secular and nonreligious. We must develop ways to reach them. Most are practical. They want to know the effects of religion in everyday life. The Adventist emphasis on health, education, and family appeals to them.

Fourth, *we must sensitively continue our mission to other Christians*. From the very beginning Adventists have had a mission to other Christians. It must remain so. That mission, however, often creates misunderstanding for both other Christians and Adventists themselves.

We have a prophetic message that must be given, but we would do well to evaluate some of our practices and attitudes. Love and a sensitiveness to the feelings of others should characterize our mission. Just as Jeremiah uttered judgment with tears (Jer. 9:1), present-day proclaimers should not speak arrogantly or vindictively. We must show sorrow about wrong and identify with those judged, as did Jeremiah. A poor attitude changes our whole perspective and turns believers away from hearing the beauty of what we preach.

Not only is Jesus the center of our message to non-Christians; He must also be centered in our message to other Christians as well. Anything special we have to say to other Christians must be directly related to Jesus, or it is less than Christian. I like to tell people that Adventism is the fullest presentation of Jesus Christ that I know. Jesus' second coming is *Jesus* coming again and a reunion with Him. The sanctuary is Jesus *now* ministering for me. Jesus is not only past but present, and future as well. Healthful living is not just a way to make me live longer, but Jesus' caring about how I feel and giving me better life. Fellow Christians want to hear not a denominational message, but a Jesus message.

The three angels' messages are a key part of the special message we are called to share. We must remember that the context of this message is about Christ also. The prelude (Rev. 14:1-6) is about the Lamb (verse 1), Jesus, and those who follow Him and are His firstfruits (verse 4).

The first angel comes with an eternal gospel or good news

169

(verse 6). The conclusion of the third angel's message calls for the endurance of the saints, who, along with keeping the commandments of God, also keep the faith of Jesus (verse 12). Jesus is the beginning and the end of the three messages.

People Matter

God has sent us. We have a powerful Jesus-centered message, but we must never forget we are sent to *people*. If we don't love them, what we say will have no effect.

For this reason we are called to minister to *all* areas of a person's life. Evangelism and caring actions go together in true mission. To offer Jesus as the Bread of Life but give no food to the hungry is not truly Christian. To dig a well for a thirsty village and not share the Water of Life is to superficially minister to only part of life.

In the end, the love demonstrated in the missionary's life has more to do with the success of gospel preaching than the clarity of theology. The messenger is the message. The missionary is the mission.

I live with a gentle woman who has never preached a sermon from the pulpit or published a religious article. She is a powerful missionary who has articulately proclaimed God's love in her quiet, unheralded way by personal word and caring act. God's earnest desire is to send all of us—male and female, talkative and quiet, all colors, shapes, sizes, and ages—into the world. He wants us to love it for Him. If we heed His *call*, we, as His church, will live!

---

* Scriptural references in this chapter are from the Revised Standard Version.

---

[1] John Foster, *Setback and Recovery* (SPCK, 1974), pp. 80, 81.
[2] *Gospel Workers*, p. 465.
[3] Figures from Ralph D. Winter at the U.S. Center for World Mission.

OUR MISSION

 John Dybdahl has been a pastor, missionary, and teacher. A graduate of Pacific Union College, Andrews University, and Fuller Theological Seminary, he has served in the Thailand Mission, Southeast Asia Union College in Singapore, and Walla Walla College. During 1989-1990 he was college developer, administrator, and teacher at Mission College in Thailand. Currently he is associate director at the Institute of World Mission at Andrews University and professor of mission in the SDA Theological Seminary.

Creation

*G*od is Creator of all things, and has revealed in Scripture the authentic account of His creative activity. In six days the Lord made "the heaven and the earth" and all living things upon the earth, and rested on the seventh day of that first week. Thus He established the Sabbath as a perpetual memorial of His completed creative work. The first man and woman were made in the image of God as the crowning work of Creation, given dominion over the world, and charged with responsibility to care for it. When the world was finished it was "very good," declaring the glory of God. (Gen. 1; 2; Ex. 20:8-11; Ps. 19-16; 33:6, 9; 104; Heb. 11:3.)—Fundamental Beliefs, *No. 6.*

CHAPTER TWENTY-ONE

By James Coffin

The Wonder of Creation
Our Source of Meaning and Self-esteem

Canvassing one day during my college years, I happened upon an articulate and outgoing man who told me he was an atheist. Despite our widely differing perspectives, we found conversation easy. Soon we were engaged in a discussion.

After considerable talk about our respective belief systems—for adamant refusal to believe is itself a *belief* system—I made the following comment: "I have on rare occasions had the thought flash momentarily into my mind, *Is it possible that maybe there really isn't a God? Is it possible that things really did come about by accident? What if Christianity is a myth?*"

Then I asked, "If I as a Christian have considered, however fleetingly, the possibility that maybe God *doesn't* exist, have you as an atheist ever wrestled, even for a few moments, with similar doubts that maybe He *does* exist?"

"Absolutely!" the man said, to my surprise. "Years ago when our first child was born I almost became a believer in God. As I looked down at that miniature-but-perfect little human being in the crib, as I watched the flexing of those tiny fingers and saw the dawning of recognition in those little eyes, I went through a period of several months during which I almost ceased to be an atheist. Looking at that child almost convinced me there had to be a God."

Even this dyed-in-the-wool atheist couldn't deny, as the psalmist had said millennia earlier, that humans are "fearfully and wonderfully made" (Ps. 139:14).* But what the atheist may have failed to realize—and indeed, what many Christians also fail to realize—is that belief in the Genesis creation account provides far

173

more than a mere explanation of how the human race came into existence. It puts into proper perspective a number of critical aspects of life. Let us look at five of these.

1. God

The Creation story describes a God who is so powerful that He needs only to *speak* and objects both living and nonliving spring into existence. As the psalmist describes it: "By the word of the Lord were the heavens made, their starry host by the breath of his mouth. . . . For he spoke, and it came to be; he commanded, and it stood firm" (Ps. 33:6-9).

Despite being so powerful that He is able to compress the creation of our entire world into six days, God is not indifferent to His creation. In fact, He derives great pleasure from it. At intervals in the creation process He reviews what has been accomplished and pronounces it good (Gen. 1:4, 10, 12, 18, 21, 25, 31). And He is particularly concerned for the happiness of humans, providing an appropriate companion for Adam as a means of forestalling loneliness.

In the Creation story we see both God's *transcendence* and His *immanence*. On the one hand is unlimited power (transcendence); on the other is friendship and intimacy (immanence). We see a God who is so awesome that the natural response is to fall on our faces before Him in fear; yet we also see a God who seeks communion with His creatures. A reading of the Creation story should prepare us for both the command to take off our shoes in God's presence (Ex. 3:5) and the command to approach Him boldly (Heb. 4:16). God is simultaneously both removed from humans and very close to us.

2. Humankind

Not only does the Creation account give us crucial insight into the nature of God, but it also places humanity in proper perspective. It removes any basis for arrogance—for no human, however brilliant or talented, even begins to approximate God. A look at God's creative acts leads us to say, as did David, "What is man that you are mindful of him, the son of man that you care for him?" (Ps. 8:4).

174

But fortunately, belief in Creation also removes any reason for low self-esteem. For while we are but the faintest shadow of what God is, just being a shadow of One so awesome is an immeasurable honor. "Let us make man in our image," God had said at our creation, "in our likeness, and let them rule over the fish of the sea and the birds of the air, over the livestock, over all the earth, and over all the creatures that move along the ground" (Gen. 1:26).

God's plan is that in the earthly sphere humans should occupy a role not altogether different from the one He occupies in the entire universe. We are to be the creative force, the rulers, the guardians, the directors. But that is not all. In Genesis 1:28 we read, "God blessed them and said to them, 'Be fruitful and increase in number; fill the earth and subdue it.' "

In a sense, God did not finish His creation—He has left that to us. God could have *filled* the earth with humans. Instead, He chose to create only two, who in turn were given the creative potential to populate the earth through a chain reaction of creativity. And even though God created Adam and Eve, He in a sense left them great latitude to also participate in creating. It was as if He provided the canvas and invited them to paint in the detail. Similarly God allows us all to develop and grow in ways of our own choosing.

As we carry on the creative process of populating the earth, He designed that we should grant similar freedoms to those we create. A father and mother pass on a genetic heritage, yet their child remains free to paint in the details. To a great degree we all determine our own character and destiny.

Creation presents the paradox of a God who is both immanent and transcendent, but it also presents the paradox of humans who must forever remain humble because we are vastly inferior to our Creator, yet who must marvel at the amazing prerogatives with which God has entrusted us.

3. Nature

Not only did God entrust humans with the stewardship of His creation, but He also created us in a manner that made us uniquely qualified to fill that role. In Genesis 2:7 we read, "The Lord God formed the man from the dust of the ground and breathed

175

into his nostrils the breath of life, and the man became a living being."

The human body is composed of the same elements as the rest of creation—carbon, oxygen, hydrogen, potassium, and a long list of other substances that high school students learn about in chemistry class. But into this mass of ordinary elements is added a special God-derived element. And the result is a being in the image of God Himself.

Humans have an affinity with Creation because we too are creatures, made of the elements common to this world. But we have a divine side that sets us apart as distinct from this world. Thus we are uniquely qualified to play our role as stewards of Creation.

Granted the obvious pleasure God derives from His creation, and granted nature's intricacy and complexity, we as humans dare not treat lightly our responsibility to oversee it. While we may differ as to the best method of achieving this goal, belief in Creation carries with it accountability for our handling of all that God has provided.

4. Marriage

Biologically, humans and many animal forms are similar. In fact, it seems that Adam became aware of the absence of a partner for himself while he was naming the various animals God had created (see Gen. 2:19, 20). However, the partner created for Adam enjoyed an intimacy not present among the animal forms.

The Bible records: "So the Lord God caused the man to fall into a deep sleep; and while he was sleeping, he took one of the man's ribs and closed up the place with flesh. Then the Lord God made a woman from the rib he had taken out of the man, and he brought her to the man. The man said, 'This is now bone of my bones and flesh of my flesh; she shall be called "woman," for she was taken out of man.' For this reason a man will leave his father and mother and be united to his wife, and they will become one flesh" (verses 21-24).

While animals are capable of reproduction, and while some animals enjoy lifelong mateship, there is nothing in the Creation account to indicate that they are capable of the level of intimacy planned for the human marriage relationship—so close that it can be described as "one flesh."

And, as many a bride and groom have been reminded during their wedding, the Creation account shows the basic equality between male and female. One is not to rule over the other. We are to enjoy a complementary relationship. We should appreciate our differences, and rest in the confidence of openness and total acceptance—for the Bible says, "The man and his wife were both naked, and they felt no shame" (verse 25).

5. The Sabbath

God's concern for His creatures led Him to set an example of balance between work and rest. The God of the universe would hardly have *needed* to rest following the six days of Creation, dramatic though they may have been. However, God knew that humans would regularly need a change of pace.

Thus the Bible says, "By the seventh day God had finished the work he had been doing; so on the seventh day he rested from all his work. And God blessed the seventh day and made it holy, because on it he rested from all the work of creating that he had done" (verses 2, 3).

Equally important as rest is the need to ensure that we not forget our roots. By establishing a weekly memorial of Creation, God has sought to remind us regularly of who we are. The Sabbath helps us to remember both the majesty and approachability of our Creator—for the Sabbath is an appointment with God. The Sabbath reminds us of both our need to be humble and our need to have self-respect—for we are sons and daughters of God (Luke 3:38).

The Sabbath holds before us our responsibility to care properly for God's creation, which He has entrusted to us. And it constantly reminds us also of the lofty ideal God has had since the beginning for the relationship between man and woman.

Getting It All Together

Too often we glibly say we believe that God created the earth, yet too seldom do we contemplate the implications of such belief.

Multitudes of humans today face an identity crisis. Who are

we? Why are we here? What is the purpose of life? The Creation account of Genesis 1 and 2 places many of the perplexities of life in the twentieth century into perspective. The Creation account tells us not only how we got here but also the high role that God intends we should play now that we are here.

---

* Bible texts in this chapter are from the New International Version.

 After being born in Iowa and growing up in Missouri, James Coffin graduated from Newbold College in England. In 1976 he entered the pastoral ministry in Australia and was ordained there. Returning to the United States, he pastored in the Chesapeake Conference before serving four years as assistant editor of *Adventist Review*. Next he worked for five years as senior editor at Signs Publishing Company in Australia. Currently he is associate pastor of the Markham Woods SDA Church in Orlando, Florida. His hobbies include sports, carpentry, travel, and writing.

The Lord's Supper

*T*he Lord's Supper is a participation in the emblems of the body and blood of Jesus as an expression of faith in Him, our Lord and Saviour. In this experience of communion Christ is present to meet and strengthen His people. As we partake, we joyfully proclaim the Lord's death until He comes again. Preparation for the Supper includes self-examination, repentance, and confession. The Master ordained the service of foot washing to signify renewed cleansing, to express a willingness to serve one another in Christlike humility, and to unite our hearts in love. The Communion service is open to all believing Christians. (1 Cor. 10:16, 17; 11:23-30; Matt. 26:17-30; Rev. 3:20; John 6:48-63; 13:1-17.)—Fundamental Beliefs, No. 15.

CHAPTER TWENTY-TWO

By John M. Fowler

The Lord's Supper
Its Message for Modern Christians

We shall now separate for the ordinance of foot washing."

The preacher finished the announcement. The procession to the ordinance of humility began as usual: men to the right, women to the left, with worshipers choosing partners as they made their way to the basins.

One man at the rear of the church caught my attention. He had come late for the service, sat on the floor, listened intently to the sermon, and taken seriously the invitation that all who have accepted Jesus could participate in the open Communion that Adventists celebrate. But he was new to the church. He knew no one. And he eagerly waited for someone to invite him to be a partner in preparation for the table.

But he seemed poor, friendless, and on the wrong side of the caste line. His position seemed desperate to himself and embarrassing to the saints in that small church in a small town in a country where caste still defines community.

I watched intently the agony etched on the face of the visitor, and waited prayerfully. Which of the saints would offer to be partner to this lonely man? The elders were busy organizing the details. The deacons were busy fetching water from the only tap outside the church. And others kept to themselves as if the visitor were not their concern.

Then suddenly the visitor did have a partner: Ravi Anandan. Ravi knelt on the cold concrete floor, gently cradled his partner's shoeless, dusty, sore-covered feet, and washed them in the clear, cool water, instantly turning it to a muddy brown. One month

181

before, Ravi would have done no such thing. He would not have allowed even the shadow of that man to come anywhere near him. To touch him would have been to touch the untouchable, an act of religious impurity and social repugnance.

What made Ravi pull down the barrier and extend the embrace? One month ago Ravi was not a Christian. But now, in his first Communion, Ravi Anandan taught me and my little church the essential meaning of the gospel and the Lord's Supper: in Jesus Christ every wall of partition comes tumbling down, and a new humanity arises for the glory of God.

The moment he looked up to the Man of the cross and accepted Him as his Saviour, Ravi Anandan knew the joy of redemption. One part of that joy is to know Jesus. The other part is to accept our fellow humans as equal to ourselves and to experience the family of God. At the cross Ravi found faith and salvation. He also learned that faith without unreserved fellowship is meaningless. And now at the Lord's table Ravi stepped across the age-old barrier of caste and prejudice and affirmed his newfound faith.

Yes, the Lord's Supper is faith's loud affirmation of a *past act,* a *present experience,* and a *future hope.* No dimension of human life escapes its scrutiny, power, or judgment. Those who participate without making such an affirmation do so in "an unworthy manner" and may be "guilty of profaning the body and blood of the Lord" (1 Cor. 11:27).*

A Past Act

When we come to the Lord's table we link ourselves together in the dynamic of redemptive history. Jesus told His disciples that the Supper is a fulfillment of the Passover (Matt. 26:17-19) and that it is the harbinger of liberation. Just as Passover symbolizes the defeat of a ruthless foe and the ushering in of freedom from bondage, so does the Supper. It is a memorial of liberation from sin and of the defeat of Creation's foe—Satan.

The Lord's Supper is an act of history. When Pilate ruled over Judea, when Annas and Caiaphas presided over the promises and the fortunes of the Jerusalem Temple, when the Man of Nazareth neared the end of His earthly life, He instituted the Lord's Supper. On the eve of the Passover, on the day before the preparation day of Passion Week, on the night He was betrayed, Jesus established the Communion service. In an upper room of a Jerusalem house, Jesus celebrated the event with the twelve, told them its meaning, and prescribed its format: He "took bread, and blessed, and broke it, and gave it to the disciples and said, 'Take, eat; this is my body.' And he took a cup, and when he had given thanks he gave it to them, saying, 'Drink of it, all of you; for this is my blood of the covenant, which is poured out for many for the forgiveness of sins' " (Matt. 26:26-28).

The Communion service is thus a fact of history. It is not a myth. It is a sacred emblem memorializing what the incarnate Lord accomplished in flesh and blood, in space and time.

The Lord's Supper is an act of redemptive history. The Last Supper was not an ordinary farewell meal of a Master who knew His end was at hand. Jesus dug deeply in the history of Israel, took the Passover symbols of bread and blood, and taught the disciples some lessons in redemptive history. When He said "Do this in remembrance of me" (1 Cor. 11:24), the Lord was asking God's people to remember at least two great truths.

First, remember the truth about sin. Sin is real. Sin is serious. Sin is costly. Sin is deadly. This needs to be said again and again, for we live in a world that looks upon sin lightly or ignores it altogether. Vivekananda, the Hindu reformist philosopher, once said that "it is a sin to call a man a sinner. It is a standing libel on human nature." [1] That may well be the view of many today—from the home of the materialist liberal to the philosophic chair of the secular humanist. But not at the table of Jesus. There we are confronted with the diabolic fact and the destructive effect of sin. It was sin that caused the cross. It was sin that broke the body of Jesus and shed His blood.

Second, remember the truth about the sacrificial death of Jesus. The Lord's Supper presents to us the "paschal lamb" (1 Cor. 5:7), "the Lamb of God, who takes away the sin of the world!" (John 1:29). When Jesus spoke of His body and blood, He referred to Calvary, where His blood would be "poured out for many for the forgiveness of sins" (Matt. 26:28).

The bread and the wine, therefore, speak to us not of His birth or life, not of His miracles or teachings, not of His example or

183

character, but of His death. It is by His death that Jesus is to be remembered. It is by His death that God reconciled "the world to himself" (2 Cor. 5:19). It is by His death that forgiveness is assured (Eph. 1:7; Col. 2:13, 14) and a common fellowship is established (Eph. 2:13-16). It is by His death that the devil is doomed (Heb. 2:14, 15).

Therefore, as often as we take part of these symbols, we give thanks and rejoice in the supreme sacrifice of the Son of God, exclaiming with John: "The blood of Jesus his Son cleanses us from all sin" (1 John 1:7).

The Lord's Supper gave to the apostolic church a sense of unity and purpose. One of the key passages that describe the dynamic of the early church is Acts 2:42: "And they devoted themselves to the apostles' teaching and fellowship, to the breaking of bread and the prayers."

The breaking of bread was a powerful, unifying tool in the early church. Jew and Gentile, male and female, slave and free, found a seat at the table and in that process discovered the oneness of Christ's body.

The table cannot be split into private seats of pride and prejudice. The table is a forceful reminder that reconciliation and racism, Christ and caste, salvation and self-centeredness, cannot live in the same heart. One or the other must yield. No wonder the apostle Paul defined the worthy Christian life as one that is "eager to maintain the unity of the Spirit in the bond of peace" (Eph. 4:3).

A Present Experience

"Do this," commanded Jesus (Luke 22:19).

In the first written account of the Lord's Supper, some 30 years after the Crucifixion, Paul charged the Corinthian church that it is fit and proper that Christians experience the joy and blessings of the Communion service (1 Cor. 11:23-29). But the experience must not become a common routine: it must be a call for self-examination, recommitment, and rejoicing.

Communion calls for self-examination. The apostle Paul warns: "Let a man examine himself, and so eat of the bread and drink of the cup. For any one who eats and drinks without discerning the body eats and drinks judgment upon himself" (verses 28, 29).

184

Examining the lives of others comes easy to all of us. But the admonition here is to examine ourselves—to place the feast of the flesh, the flight of the reason, and the flaw of our own souls under the scrutiny of the broken body and the shed blood.

What is the state of my Christian experience? How has my life been in comparison to the events of the "night when he was betrayed"? Have I walked with Him, talked with Him, studied His Word, as I should have? Have I sought God's grace to overcome sin—not just the great sins against God but also those little sins that revolve around relationships with people who are different from me, with people who live with me, with people who work or worship with me?

The wavering Peter, the ambitious John, the angry James, the timid Andrew, the shy Bartholomew, the doubting Thomas, the crooked Judas, and others at the table asked the question "Is it I, Lord?" (Matt. 26:22). I am no better than they and need to ask that question too. Is it possible that I have betrayed the Lord in some way?

We call the Lord's Supper the Communion, but is communion possible without togetherness with God, with one another? Estranged relationship is Satan's anthem of doubt on the power of the gospel to reconcile. Before we sit at the table of Christian brotherhood, we must let brotherhood do its ministry of love and reconciliation. That's why Jesus commanded the disciples: "If I then, your Lord and Teacher, have washed your feet, you also ought to wash one another's feet. For I have given you an example" (John 13:14, 15).

The towel is a symbol of humility and service—the condescension of divinity into human flesh in order that God may accomplish His cosmic purposes in the plan of redemption. In taking that towel, we too participate in an incarnate ministry to the poorest of the poor, to the lonely, to the neglected, to the weary, to the unwanted, and to those who may despise us. The ordinance "is to clear away . . . misunderstandings, to bring man out of his selfishness, down from his stilts of self-exaltation, to the humility of heart that will lead him to serve his brother." [2]

Communion calls for recommitment. We come to the table not

185

only to commemorate, not only to self-examine, but to recommit ourselves to the crucified Lord.

Jesus pictured this need for daily recommitment and surrender through the forceful imagery we find in John's Gospel: "Unless you eat the flesh of the Son of man and drink his blood, you have no life in you; he who eats my flesh and drinks my blood has eternal life" (John 6:53, 54). The misunderstanding of passages like this led to the accusation that the first-century Christians were a mystic cult practicing some sort of cannibalism. But the meaning of the passage is clear from the verse that follows: "He who eats my flesh and drinks my blood abides in me, and I in him" (verse 56).

Abiding! We in Him. He in us. That's the challenge of the Lord's Supper. "To eat the flesh and drink the blood of Christ is to receive Him as a personal Saviour, believing that He forgives our sins, and that we are complete in Him. . . . We must feed upon Him, receive Him into the heart, so that His life becomes our life. His love, His grace, must be assimilated." [3]

Communion calls for thanksgiving and rejoicing. Ellen White describes the Communion service as Christ's own appointment where He "meets His people, and energizes them by His presence." [4]

There at the table Jesus reminds us of our assurance of forgiveness and gives us a reason to rejoice and be thankful. Bread, wine, and a song to conclude the meal tells us that in Jesus we have victory and joy. He is our bread. He is our life. He is our new covenant. He is our song.

Rejoice, therefore, in the forgiveness of sins. Rejoice in the reality of reconciliation. Rejoice in the power of the abiding Christ. And rejoice for the nearness of the day when we shall sit at the Lord's table with Him at the head.

A Future Hope

As He concluded the supper Jesus made a promise: "I shall not drink again of this fruit of the vine until that day when I drink it new with you in my Father's kingdom" (Matt. 26:29). The apostle Paul reminded the Corinthians that "as often as you eat this bread and drink the cup, you proclaim the Lord's death until he comes" (1 Cor. 11:26).

THE LORD'S SUPPER

The Communion service is thus a tangible symbol—something we feel, taste, and touch—of something sacred, mysterious, and majestic. It links history, existence, and hope. It points back to the cross, affirms the meaning of life today, and directs our attention to the "marriage supper of the Lamb" (Rev. 19:9).

In that hope we must live. The Adventist life is a life of hope—a hope based on the cross, a hope that God will soon transform this world, burn up every trace of tragedy, wipe away every tear, cure every shattered life, mend the brokenhearted, and place us all at His feet forever in the enduring presence of heaven's new dawn.

---

* Bible texts in this chapter are taken from the Revised Standard Version.

---

[1] Swami Vivekananda, *Speeches and Writings,* 3rd ed. (Madras, India: G. A. Natesan, n.d.), p. 39.
[2] *The Desire of Ages,* p. 650.
[3] *Ibid.,* p. 389.
[4] *Ibid.,* p. 656.

Born and reared in India, John M. Fowler has a long and varied career with the church. It includes, in part, being a pastor, a teacher, chief editor at the Oriental Watchman Publishing House in Poona, India, and associate secretary of the Southern Asia Division. Fowler has had more than 150 articles in denominational magazines. He has been a guest lecturer at Spicer Memorial College and has served as adjunct professor at Andrews University. He is currently associate editor of *Ministry.*

# The Nature of Man

*M*an and woman were made in the image of
God with individuality, the power and freedom to think and to do. Though created free
beings, each is an indivisible unity of body, mind, and spirit, de-
pendent upon God for life and breath and all else. When our first
parents disobeyed God, they denied their dependence upon Him
and fell from their high position under God. The image of God in
them was marred and they became subject to death. Their descendants share this fallen nature and its consequences. They are
born with weaknesses and tendencies to evil. But God in Christ
reconciled the world to Himself and by His Spirit restores in pen-
itent mortals the image of their Maker. Created for the glory of
God, they are called to love Him and one another, and to care for
their environment. (Gen. 1:26-28; 2:7; Ps. 8:4-8; Acts 17:24-28;
Gen. 3; Ps. 51:5; Rom. 5:12-17; 2 Cor. 5:19, 20; Ps. 51:10;
1 John 4:7, 8, 11, 20; Gen. 2:15.)—Fundamental Beliefs, No. 7.

Who Are We?
The Mystery of Our Creation and Destiny

Some years back, I was serving on a committee whose task it was to make editorial revisions to a document for school accreditation purposes. When I suggested that our language be gender-inclusive wherever possible, one colleague objected half-jokingly by stating that the document would get "messy" if we started writing "his/her" everywhere. Looking back on that experience makes me think how much "neater" things would be if humans were of only one gender. Nevertheless, humans are male and female, and that was God's "messy" idea, not ours!

Keeping that plurality at the forefront of our thinking will assist us in understanding the underlying miracle of human creation by an all-knowing and relentlessly loving God.

God as Love

To understand the nature of humans, one must begin with God as love. Human beings are much more than mere reproductive machines whose destiny is to multiply and fill the earth. The Godhead, in loving consultation, chose to make us like Themselves: free-willed, thinking agents capable of moral decision-making and bound to one another in love (be it romantic, filial, or spiritual love). To be human is to be empowered by God Himself to think and do according to human will as well as God's. The ideal set forth for all is that those wills will be in perfect harmony so that doing our will is, in fact, fulfilling the divine.

In the Genesis account we are made aware of the collaborative nature of the Creation venture only as we are suddenly allowed to

189

eavesdrop on the Godhead, as it were, as They mutually agree on an important decision: "Let us make man in our image" (Gen. 1:26). The Creation account in Genesis 1 underscores the Trinity's intention, right from the outset, to create man as well as woman together. The account in Genesis 2 tells us that the male came forth out of the dust. He was not called forth by word, as had the other entities of Creation. Rather, Adam was "formed," the word coming from the Hebrew *yatsar,* which means "to squeeze into shape, to mold, to fashion [as in pottery]." In other words, we are God's work of art!

Born of the Earth, Not by Word

So man and woman were not created ex nihilo (by word, out of nothing), like the rest of creation. God, like a cosmic sculptor, chose to make humans out of previously created material. Why? I believe it was that we should understand that we belong irrevocably to the rest of creation by virtue of the matter from which we came. We belong to the earth and to one another. Once all His creation was finished, God was able to declare that this arrangement was "very good" (Gen. 1:31).

Created Male and Female

The human pair was created different but equal. Their difference, moreover, made them interdependent and complementary. Woman was created from the dust indirectly through the rib of the man so that their mutual completeness inside the love relationship might be underscored.

Being created in the image of God implied both individuality and relationship, just as God is at once one and plural. Human plurality guaranteed the operation of love, and love was to characterize the relationship of the two. It is important, then, that God should put man to sleep during the woman's creation. Man was never to feel responsible for creating woman. The creation of woman, like that of man, was to be by the express will of God—for His own purpose and His own glory. It was only at the Fall that the God-ordained balance in male-female relations was thrown into disorder. Even so, the plan of redemption restores the mutuality and complementarity of human relations (between the sexes, races, and classes) through the doctrine of our oneness in Jesus Christ (Gal. 3:28).

So the human race at its inception consisted of two individual beings created from and in the image of one divine Source, similar yet different in physical, intellectual, and spiritual abilities and needs, and destined to reflect the loving, moral character of God. Male and female in their original and redeemed form (both ideal states) are complementary and equal in their relationship and respectful of their own and each other's individuality.

Unity in Plurality

Each human being is an organic unity of body, soul, and spirit. At Creation man and woman were formed out of dust and then filled with "the breath of life." The ensuing product was a "living soul" (Gen. 2:7).

The phrase "living soul" *(nephesh, chaiyah)* points to human existence as a summation of physical body and breath of divine origin. And "soul" here refers to the individual human existing in his/her individuality as a separate, unique unit of life. The soul, far from being a part of the individual, constitutes the very person himself/herself. There can be no "person" without the combination of body and *nephesh* (or *psuche,* the Greek equivalent of *nephesh).*

The other player in the human trinity (body, soul, spirit) that makes up the individual is *ruach,* the Hebrew word translated most often as "spirit," "wind," or "breath." As breath it refers both to animals and humans. At death the *ruach* leaves the body (Ps. 146:4) and returns to its Maker (Eccl. 12:7). As in the case of *nephesh* or *psuche, ruach* does not have a living, conscious existence apart from the physical body. This meaning is borne out in the Greek term *pneuma,* which derives from the verb *pneo,* to "blow or breathe."

In other words, the same unity and diversity we witness in the Godhead and that we see replicated in the male-female relationship is mirrored in the tripartite unity of the human being. Paul's reference to the completeness of the individual as spirit, soul, and body is in harmony with the overall biblical understanding of our makeup. "Now," he said, "may the God of peace Himself sanctify you completely; and may your whole spirit, soul, and body be preserved blameless at the coming of our Lord Jesus Christ" (1 Thess. 5:23, NKJV). If we were to visualize these concepts, they might look like this:

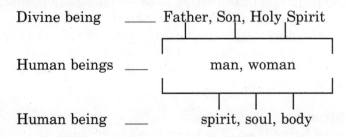

Divine being ____ Father, Son, Holy Spirit

Human beings ____ man, woman

Human being ____ spirit, soul, body

Sin broke up this harmony of trinities and attempted to destroy once and for all the life-giving relationship between creature and the Creator.

Love's Risks

One can hardly imagine a plan more beautiful than the one outlined in Genesis 1 and the first half of Genesis 2. Man and woman created in the physical and moral image of a loving God. Even after their fall into sin, the psalmist could say about them that they were made only "a little lower than the angels ["than God" in some versons]" (Ps. 8:6).

Why did God want to create such beings if He knew that they could use their freedom of choice to reject Him? It seems evident that the very character of God, His infinite love, demanded such an act. Love longs to communicate on a giving-receiving model, and the more it does, the greater its need to share this communion. Creation is the most logical outgrowth of love because it allows that life-giving communion that God meant to have with humans.

But through the malignity of an angelic being gone wrong, the principle of selfishness and isolation came to replace the principle of love at the core of human beings. Lucifer, an angel creature of the highest order, gifted with many talents as long as he remembered the source of his beauty and abilities, had the privilege of remaining within God's love relationship. But when he willfully forgot the Source of his excellence, it became increasingly intolerable for him to express love, and even more painful to receive it. Ezekiel 28:17 states that it was pride that undid this privileged being, and Isaiah implies that he began to think that he should occupy God's place (Isa. 14:12-14). Eventually his disruptive choices, with its resulting behavior, placed him beyond the reach of love, and he and his followers were cast out of heaven (Rev. 12:4, 7-9).

As the originator of sin on earth, Lucifer now became Satan, the accuser—that "old serpent" who ends up in the lake of fire. It was Satan in the form of a seductive serpent who insinuated to the woman in Eden that she did not need her relationship with God. Could it be, he suggested, that she might be happier outside this choking relationship?

Similar thoughts were insinuated into the man's mind when he was presented with the opportunity to use his will in a manner equally and tantalizingly truant. Adam began to wonder, no doubt, if he had more power than God had led him to believe. In the end he made a conscious decision to abandon the unwritten but clearly understood covenant of love that he and Eve had with God and with each other. Once broken, their relationship of trust and mutual admiration crumbled into fear, distrust, and recrimination. And God became to them a Person to be feared and despised as their growing guilt made them look for a scapegoat.

Sin Fractures Relationship

Sin, then, was and continues to be the willful severing of a love relationship with God. Since God is love (1 John 4:8), to break off our relationship with Him is to enter automatically into a loveless path that leads eventually to moral and physical death. But moral death comes first. It reveals itself in an array of thoughts, desires, and behaviors that are not only unworthy of humans made in the image of God, but that work against their own mental and moral health and destroy all relationships, human and divine. It is a miserable, lonely path of self-serving and self-indulgence at the expense of self-worth. It is a power struggle at the expense of inner peace, and it leads to guilt-ridden isolation and centripetal self-destruction.

Adam and Eve could not have imagined the implications of

their choice, and we might even commiserate with this tragic pair who walked innocently into the devil's trap. What hope could there be for the guilty couple but to accept the inevitable disastrous results of their decisions?

But that question was answered by the "Lamb slain before the foundation of the world" (Rev. 13:8). The promise of restoration made to them in their most desperate hour of need also passed on to their progeny: "And I will put enmity between thee and the woman, and between thy seed and her seed; it shall bruise thy head, and thou shalt bruise his heel" (Gen. 3:15). The Seed of the woman, Jesus Christ, the Son of God, would come to heal the broken love relationship between humanity and God and one another.

The Road Back to Love

God's forgiveness opens the way for human forgiveness and lasting restoration: "God was in Christ, reconciling the world unto himself" (2 Cor. 5:19). But how does fallen human nature come to the point where it senses its need of salvation and healing? The story of the prodigal son illustrates our redemption in Christ. The younger son of the generous father decided to claim his inheritance and made off with it to a foreign land to live as he pleased. Growing increasingly isolated from himself and others in his wanton living, he ended up in a pigsty, feeling hungry and deserted.

Coming to his senses, he first thought about a person—his kindly father. Why? Because love and life have to do with relationships. To break a relationship of love, one must silence conscience and virtue. The opposite of sin is not simply holiness, but wholeness; not simply righteousness, but right relations. And the young man did not feel whole until he had returned to his father and healed his own and his father's broken heart.

The prodigal son's desperate state made him begin to think about his father. But in fact, it was the call of Divinity through his pain that made him reconsider his life. It is the way God wins us over, by persuading us lovingly and persistently through conscience, tragedy, artistic or musical beauty, the kindness of a person—whatever means that will awaken us from the stupor of sin. Indeed, sin is a form of death—people who have experienced

194

conversion talk of noticing a sunrise or a tree growing near their home for the first time. They suddenly notice the physical or moral beauty of a person very close to them, a person who, before their spiritual awakening, seemed dull or even hostile.

With Jesus, love is given its rightful place at the center of human existence and being, and the human trinity of body, soul, and spirit come into perfect sychronization with the divine Trinity.

The Trinity, in turn, works endlessly to maintain that harmony within the individual and in the individual's relationships with others. There is only one covenant, and that is the eternal covenant of love. It teaches us that through the working of God's love in our lives, each willing man or woman can enjoy a new nature, one that is fed by divine love and that acts out the dictates of that love in daily life.

Renewed human nature is not the work of humans, but of the Godhead, the Creator of life and love at Creation. The daily submission of the will through faith is the only "work" that is needed to receive the benefits of forgiveness, healing, and full restoration.

Lourdes E. Morales-Gudmundsson, Ph.D., is professor of Spanish at the University of Connecticut, Storrs, Connecticut. She is president of Palabras deVida, Inc. (Words of Life, Inc.), a non-profit organization whose television program by the same name will be broadcast this year. Professor Morales-Gudmundsson is a member of various NAD committees, including the Board of Higher Education and Hispanic Higher Education and Advisory Committee.

Marriage and the Family

Marriage was divinely established in Eden and affirmed by Jesus to be a lifelong union between a man and a woman in loving companionship. For the Christian a marriage commitment is to God as well as to the spouse, and should be entered into only between partners who share a common faith. Mutual love, honor, respect, and responsibility are the fabric of this relationship, which is to reflect the love, sanctity, closeness, and permanence of the relationship between Christ and His church. Regarding divorce, Jesus taught that the person who divorces a spouse, except for fornication, and marries another, commits adultery. Although some family relationships may fall short of the ideal, marriage partners who fully commit themselves to each other in Christ may achieve loving unity through the guidance of the Spirit and the nurture of the church. God blesses the family and intends that its members shall assist each other toward complete maturity. Parents are to bring up their children to love and obey the Lord. By their example and their words they are to teach them that Christ is a loving disciplinarian, ever tender and caring, who wants them to become members of His body, the family of God. Increasing family closeness is one of the earmarks of the final gospel message. (Gen. 2:18-25; Matt. 19:3-9; John 2:1-11; 2 Cor. 6:14; Eph. 5:21-33; Matt. 5:31, 32; Mark 10:11, 12; Luke 16:18; 1 Cor. 7:10, 11; Ex. 20:12; Eph. 6:1-4; Deut. 6:5-9; Prov. 22:6; Mal. 4:5, 6.)—Fundamental Beliefs, No. 22.

CHAPTER TWENTY-FOUR
By Karen and Ron Flowers

The Adventist Family
An Incubation for Faith

O
ur son caught me collapsed in my overstuffed chair with a book, looking for inspiration for this chapter. A book called *What Is a Family?* Now, this boy has always had the capacity to reduce things to prime. "What is a family?" he read incredulously off the spine. "Mom, you mean you don't know the answer to that by now?"

It's true we've been husband and wife nearly 27 years, parents for better than 21, a son and a daughter for nearly a half century. We also have experience at most of the other garden-variety family relationships. About all that's left for us to brave is being the in-laws ourselves and grandparenting. Even if you don't consider a decade and a half of work in family ministries, it's logical we should know something. Yet every time I sit down in front of the computer, it's not easy to put family ministries on paper. The temptation is to write a selective piece on the joys of family living, something akin to the Christmas letters we send and receive every year. But there is something about the reality around me that begs for honesty and more than an overdose of platitudes.

The kids left yesterday to go back to school after a break. It's a time when folks take stock. Both the refrigerator and (at last!) the laundry room are empty. There's a wide ring in the tub; even the dog needs a bath. It was good to have them home, but waving goodbye also has its measure of relief. Perhaps we're just getting too old for all this frenzied activity.

Or perhaps having them home makes it harder to push concerns about them out of our minds. They're old enough now to

197

make most of their own decisions. Some are really big decisions that will affect them for a lifetime. Have we said enough? too much? I lie awake sometimes rehearsing the things I'd like to say. Wishing I could know what they're thinking, and wishing at the same time I could write their response. Sorry we've said and done things over the years that block openness and vulnerability.

Marriage has at best been on hold for a few weeks. We were asked today to complete a test to evaluate the strengths and struggles of our relationship. I wonder, as I fill out my computer score card, how he will respond, on a scale of one to five, to statements like "It is very easy for me to express all my true feelings to my partner"; "My partner is often critical and makes comments that put me down"; "I do not share some things with my partner because I am afraid he/she will get angry"; "My partner has all the qualities I've always wanted in a mate."

I talked an hour long-distance to my "little" brother last night. We laughed about my pushing 50 and his pushing 40, and how neither landmark seems so old anymore. I smiled later to myself about the different things growing up brings to relationships. I can't remember the last time we said, "I love you." Deep down we always have, but it felt good to say so; it was nice to hear. My brother doesn't worship in an Adventist church right now. Some things are harder to talk about.

Hurting people have moved in and out of my days this week. People I care about. People who are struggling with relationships. People who have personal issues to unravel because of hard experiences at the hands of those whom they were supposed to be able to trust to love them. Family.

No, my son, there's a depth to the meaning of family that defies a hasty "everybody knows that" brush-off. There's more to be probed than the vague assertion that of course family is something we all believe in, like we're all for motherhood and apple pie. Else, I find myself musing, why would our church list "family" among its 27 most fundamental beliefs, with so much else vying for such venerated status? To wrestle that elusive something concretely to the mat is the challenge of this AnchorPoint.

Many answers to the question "What is a family?" could be given that would be good and worth thinking about. But the answer we seek as Adventists securing anchor points is one that constitutes bedrock, the very essence of this thing called "family" that has spiritual significance. Does family belong among fundamental beliefs because Scripture has more to say about it than some other subjects? Is its long history as an institution its only title to lasting significance? Is our basic purpose to carefully define "family" as a noun, to delineate the proper players and their precise roles? Are family relationships primarily of concern to a remnant people because they are perceived to mark the last frontier of personal holiness to be conquered along the sanctification trail?

Or is there fundamental belief bedrock about the meaning and purpose of family to be found beneath the surface shale that lies at the foundation of all that it means to be fully human, created in the image of God, born for intimacy both with Him and with one another? Bedrock that forms the indispensable underpinnings for both discipleship and disciplemaking? We believe the answer to this last question is yes, and would have been yes even if earth were still Eden. Like all pristine truth, this family bedrock embodies the ideals toward which we stretch, all that Christians will want to know about God's "very good" design. Reason enough for a place among the 27.

But in a treatise on family ideals, there will be one crucial factor that remains unaccounted for. This bedrock has been violently disrupted, viciously turned on end, savagely altered by one cataclysmic element—sin. Where once family had been a lavish wellspring of wholeness, intimacy, joy, in sin's ironic twist family has become a polluted well whose waters can no longer be counted on to run clear and clean, where to draw water at all is to risk brokenness, disconnectedness, and pain. Even among Adventists who smile in their pews on Sabbath morning, family for many is synonymous with abuse, dysfunction, turmoil, and despair. For some, the personal devastation linked with family experience has been so withering there can be no smiles, pews may be empty, and even the healing cascade of God's grace seems beyond reach.

The good news is that Scripture on family is no stranger to brokenness. Circumscribed in its pages are both the way the world is and the way it should be. There are ideals like stars to steer by, unchanging in their courses, steady, sure sources of light and bearing. But there are also real people who have sailed the rough seas of life where we sail them, that we might have hope.[1] There is a first message that upholds all that God wants for His children, but there is also a second message of healing grace and new beginnings. The Adventist family anchor must always be cast with two ropes if it is to steady the ship in the storm—one securely fastened to the ideals, the other in firm touch with the reality of the full spectrum of human life on a broken planet and God's grace, which alone can make it bearable.

We believe there are at least three significant truths integral to a Seventh-day Adventist fundamental belief about family:

1. Family is central to health and happiness for human beings because we are created for relationships. Our Creator is a personal being who seeks fellowship with His creation, and from the beginning He implanted a desire for companionship at the core of our being as well. Marriage and children are integral to God's general plan for family. It is the setting provided by God for the meeting of our deepest intimacy needs and the perpetuation of the human race. But knowing that even at best no single family unit can meet all the intimacy needs of its members, that the load would be too heavy to bear, and that at worst many families would never know intimacy at all, our all-wise God provided for friendship and support in the larger family circle of the church.

On a planet growing ever more densely populated and crowded, it seems a paradox that many feel lonely and isolated. The great tragedy comes when the church begins to simulate the world at large. For even as sin creates enormous barriers to intimacy between us, the fact does not change that we need each other, that none of us is so strong and independent as not to need love, intimacy, and dialogue in community. And God has given us a responsibility for one another. Remembering we are family both at home and in the church must keep us trying to find ways to get gut-level real with each other. Knowing we are family must keep us seeking to learn how to mediate healing grace to one another before any more of us are tempted to try going it alone because going it together seems so far out of our grasp.

2. Family is for every human being born—the incubator for

200

faith. James Fowler, in his classic work on faith development, *Stages of Faith,* asserts that all human beings develop faith. But faith is not a term simply synonymous either with religion or belief. Rather, a person's faith is defined by his or her response to the key questions of faith: "On what or whom do you set your heart? To what vision of right-relatedness between humans, nature and the transcendent are you loyal? What hope and what ground of hope animate you and give shape to the force field of your life and to how you move into it?" [2] Faith is not primarily a static noun, but rather a dynamic verb. It is what helps us make sense of and gives direction to the experiences of life. It defines what we ultimately value and place our trust in and what is the surety for that trust.

Faith itself, says Fowler, is always relational. "There is always *another* in faith," someone or something "I trust in and am loyal to." [3] Further, faith is formed in the context of community. The first search for significant others in whom to trust is in the family. As God would have it, as children are attached to the family with bonds of love and care, a loyalty is formed as well to shared family beliefs and values, the family's view of God and truth. Only in the later stages of faith development will these values be owned individually. And even then, in God's design they are to be lived out and passed on in community, in a braided cord of families that stretches across generations, both at home and in the church.

Ellen White encapsulates the thought when she says that children's "whole religious experience is affected by their bringing up in childhood." [4] This is true because family is the primary setting in which the capacity for intimacy is developed, for better or for worse. And because knowing how to be intimate both with God and with each other is what being a disciple and making a disciple are all about (see John 15:15; 13:35). Armand Nicholi, a Christian psychiatrist of Harvard Medical School, expands: "Early family experience determines our adult character structure, the inner picture we harbor of ourselves, how we see others and feel about them, our concept of right and wrong, our capacity to establish the close, warm, sustained relationships necessary to have a family of our own, our attitude toward authority and toward the Ultimate Authority in our lives, and the way we attempt to make sense out of our existence. No human interaction has a greater impact on our lives than our family experience." [5]

So that's the ideal. In a sense it's also the real, because these are the laws of human faith development we are talking about. But there's another reality we must confront, and that is that the energies of many adults are being absorbed just coping with the brokenness of their lives that are rooted in painful family experiences. Energies that cannot be drawn upon to disciple their own children or for Christian witness. Remembering we are family means we must commit ourselves to helping one another become whole so we will have something to give to mission.

3. Jesus said that how we do relationships is the demonstration that counts of the reality and substance of our faith. Family is not only the place where disciples are made; being family is itself discipleship. It is through love for one another that we manifest love for God. When Jesus painted a picture of the end-time, He portrayed saints surprised to find themselves counted among the righteous, asking why. God responds, "As you did it [showed love] to one of the least of these my brethren, you did it to me" (Matt. 25:40, RSV). The surest proof of our acceptance of Christ's atoning righteousness will be how we have let Him make us loving and lovable Christians. Through us all, God wants to show His love to the world. Countless people around us long for a vision of His love. They search for models of what it means to be a Christian family. They hunger for human affection and embrace. Jesus' question penetrates the centuries: "You are the world's seasoning, to make it tolerable. If you lose your flavor, what will happen to the world?" (Matt. 5:13, TLB).

So where does all this leave families with kids growing up and marriage struggles and rings in the bathtub? Families with members off on their own searches for faith? Families in such pain they can scarcely hang on to hope? And Adventists looking for anchor points? It leaves us knowing, on the one hand, that there is no more significant fundamental belief in our list than the one about family, because if family fails, we have lost both our best hope for the inculcation of all the rest, and we have lost our greatest witness. It's worth our best energies to make it work.

But on the other hand, it can leave us frightened and discouraged because few of us delude ourselves that we are "making it work" with any semblance of perfection. Unless we remind each other that the surety of our faith rests in Jesus, in whose perfection alone we have hope. And that perhaps the most important things we all need to learn in the family are what Christians do when they have made mistakes, when anger has gotten out of hand, when hurtful things have been said and done, when relationships have drifted apart, when love has not been enough. Remembering we are family means we have made covenant to walk the path toward healing together, to be there for each other when it seems all else has failed, though it will stretch human commitment to the limit. And when, for some, brokenness and pain run so deep that they cannot seem to lay hold of grace, when relationships have become so destructive that they can no longer endure, remembering we are a big family means we must not compound their pain with judgment and the casting of blame. Ours is to reach out a hand in love, to support and encourage, to bind up broken hearts.

Something in me likes neat packages. Ideals are like that. Real life has too many loose ends. It will be eternity before some things are tied up with a bow. But we can hold on. We're family.

---

[1] See *Testimonies,* vol. 4, p. 12.

[2] James W. Fowler, *Stages of Faith* (New York: Harper & Row, 1981), p. 14.

[3] *Ibid.,* p. 16.

[4] *Child Guidance,* p. 473.

[5] Armand Nicholi II, "The Fractured Family: Following It Into the Future," *Christianity Today,* May 25, 1979, p. 11.

Karen and Ron Flowers are directors of family ministries at the General Conference. They have presented family enrichment seminars in more than 40 countries and have published numerous training manuals for local church family ministries. They live with their two college-age sons, Jeff and Jon, in Takoma Park, Maryland.

ALSO BY THESE AUTHORS

Roy Adams
  The Sanctuary

Rosa Taylor Banks, ed.
  A Woman's Place

Charles E. Bradford
  *The Wit and Wisdom of
    Charles Bradford*

Richard M. Davidson
  A Love Song for the Sabbath

Jon Dybdahl
  Missions: A Two-Way Street
  Old Testament Grace

Karen and Ron Flowers
  Love Aflame

John W. Fowler
  Adventist Pastoral Ministry

Clifford Goldstein
  1844 Made Simple
  Best Seller
  False Balances
  Hands Across the Gulf
  How Dare You Judge Us, God?
  A Pause for Peace
  The Saving of America

William G. Johnsson
  Behold His Glory
  Blessed Assurance
  I Chose Adventism
  In Absolute Confidence
  *Why I Am a Seventh-day
    Adventist*
  Wising Up
  *The Wit and Wisdom of
    Charles Bradford (editor)*

Marvin Moore
  The Crisis of the End Time
  The Refiner's Fire
  When Religion Doesn't Work
  Witnesses Through Trial

Monte Sahlin
  *Sharing Our Faith With
    Friends Without Losing
    Either*

Alden Thompson
  Inspiration

Arnold V. Wallenkampf
  From Rebellion to Restoration

Martin Weber
  Adventist Hot Potatoes
  *Hurt, Healing, and Happy
    Again*
  More Adventist Hot Potatoes
  My Tortured Conscience
  Some Call It Heresy

The Master's Touch

by Charles Mills

ADVENTISTS SHARE EXCITING STORIES OF GOD'S LEADING

Amazing! Astounding! Unbelievable! Common words used to describe what it's like when God directly intervenes in a person's life. *The Master's Touch*, third book in the best-selling *Paint the World With Love* series, reveals how ordinary Adventists all across North America have come in contact with God's love in some very extraordinary ways.

If you've ever wondered if God still touches lives today, here's your answer!

Paper, 128 pages. US$8.95, Cdn$12.10.

A Remnant in Crisis

by Jack W. Provonsha

Has the Adventist Church lost its sense of mission? Does its message still have a cutting edge? Dr. Jack Provonsha shows that the unique synthesis of truth centered in the three angels' message has special relevance for society today.

Through a fresh analysis of our doctrines of Creation, the Sabbath, health, holiness, even the investigative judgment, he directs readers to a rediscovery of our mission.

Hardcover with dust jacket, 173 pages. US$14.95, Cdn$20.20.